Praise 1

"Simple, powerful truths and insightful reflections from Raz Chan, whose mastery of martial arts infuses a compelling narrative, tracing a life from a child's wonder and a teenager's insecurity, to an adult's realization that ambition should be learned, taught and celebrated.

An inspired man of ideas, Sensei Chan's words are shaped by oral traditions from the East and informed by a Western enthusiasm for stories of personal pursuit. Raz is a warrior, a teacher and a gentleman."

- **Michael French, Producer,** *Heart of a Dragon & Jim Carey: Unnatural Act*

"For the past year I have known Raz Chan as a superior Martial Arts teacher and mentor; I am pleased to also know him as an author. The Human Excellence Project is an exceptional book that will help you bring renewed focus and vision to your life. It is clear, accessible, compelling, and inspiring."

- **Dr. David Klonsky, Professor of Psychology, University of British Columbia**

"Highly recommended for executives, parents, and athletes who would like to increase their success and fulfillment."

- **Colin Sprake, Author of Entrepreneur Success Recipe**

The Human Excellence Project

The Human Excellence Project:

Lessons Even Awesome Parents Never Teach

*"I don't build world champions...
I build life champions."*

- Sensei Raz Chan

Copyright © 2016 Raz Chan International

All rights reserved.

ISBN: 978-0-9951733-0-9

DEDICATION

To the millions of people around world searching for their life purpose and achieving their greatest dreams. To the betterment of lives of everyone.

CONTENTS

	Acknowledgements	vii
	Introduction	1
1	Patience	16
2	Responsibility	23
3	Passion	30
4	Awareness	41
5	Respect	50
6	Focus	55
7	Discipline	69
8	Confidence	76
9	Positive Attitude	85
10	Vision	95
11	Leadership	102
12	Humility	106
13	Courage	113
14	Honor	119
15	Listen	133
16	Presence	139
	About the Author	158

Acknowledgments

There are key people who come into your life over the years, transforming you into something meaningful and special. I would like to thank these people because without them I would not be writing this today nor doing what I love to do for a career.

My parents, James and Donna Chan for teaching me what it takes to succeed in life and business. The hard life lessons I learned from them have kept me focused in times of challenge.

To my loving wife of 12 years Linda, thank you for your support in my entrepreneurial ventures.

Special thanks to all my clients from Raz Chan Fitness, especially the ones from the women's cardio kickboxing program. It is you ladies who allowed me to leave my corporate job in 2005 to become a full-time entrepreneur. Without you, I would not have accomplished this dream.

Last but not least, I want to thank my mentors: Colin Sprake of Make Your Mark Training who shifted my thinking to become more global with my business aspirations. To my Brazilian Jiu-Jitsu teacher Todd Nathanson for teaching me what it means to be a great black belt.

The Human Excellence Project

Introduction

THE FIRST FEW YEARS of my life in Winnipeg, Manitoba were very happy times. Like most kids I was carefree, expressive, and had a zest for life. Everything was awesome in my world. My family was living with my grandparents at the time and the household was full of happiness. It helped that my cousins and siblings were all roughly the same age so we were constantly chasing one another around the house.

My grandparents couldn't have been happier seeing their grandkids enjoying their daily rampage through their house. It was happy times for the Chan family. Life seemed great and there was no reason to believe life would not continue this way for the foreseeable future.

In 1976, my parents moved into their own home not too far away from my grandparents. For the first year, there was little change, with the exception I didn't see my cousins as frequently; other than that, nothing seemed out of place. It was my first year in kindergarten. Some of the kids were struggling with separation anxiety constantly crying for their mothers when they were dropped off, but not me. As soon as my mom let go of my hand, I ran toward the other children to play. Up to that point in my life I was carefree and fearless.

I didn't know a word of English as my parents and relatives communicated to me in Cantonese in my pre-school years. A few days later, I began to experience behavior from other kids that would set the stage of how my experience in school will be till the end of the high school.

One day as the teacher gathered us around in a circle for storytelling time, a girl by the name of Michelle was sitting in front of me. She casually turned around, stared at me, and placed two fingers by the side of her eyes slanting the corner of her eyes upward. At first, I wasn't sure what she meant but quickly realized she was mocking the shape of my Chinese eyes.

I was only 6 years old at the time and never encountered racism in my neighborhood. Perhaps it was because my social world revolved around my cousins and siblings. I sat there in shock, unable to explain why someone would do that to me. I was just trying to make friends, and was not hurting anyone. My parents always taught me to be respectful to everyone in order to be treated in the same way in return. I was puzzled - if that were the case, then why had this happened to me. I'd always lived in a black and white world. You were either good or bad but not in between. Maybe that is why I became a martial artist. The principles of respect for yourself and others resonated with me.

Little did I know that this one racist gesture would not be the last one for me. In fact, racism became a regular occurrence throughout my school years - sometime directly and other times indirectly. I was different and some of the kids and even the adults would make sure I was not welcomed.

At least my home would be my sanctuary, or so I thought. Shortly, after my parents moved into our new home they began to argue over money. In the beginning, the arguments were sporadic. It was difficult seeing two people who apparently love each other be so destructive. Seeing my parents fight for the first time was a brand new experience for me. I didn't know what to think of it but it wasn't a regular occurrence in our first year at the new home so it quickly faded from memory after the incident was resolved.

As I began the first grade, things started to unravel in our household and at school. I began to notice my mother constantly asking my father for grocery money with an urgent tone. When I was tucked into bed at night, all was quiet until my father came home just after midnight from his shift at the restaurant. Outside of my bedroom door I could hear discussions between my mother and father. It started out quietly to not disturb the kids, but would escalate into heated arguments lasting until the early morning.

This would be life in our household until I left at the age of 23: turbulent, volatile, toxic, and negative. After each argument, my mother would sit me down at the kitchen table telling me to not be like my father. He's a bad man, she would say.

It was hard to hear that and I did not want to accept it. Why me I would ask? Why couldn't my family be normal like the rest of kids in the neighborhood? Yes, my father made mistakes but he was not involved with crime and God forbid it was not like he was some axe murderer. Unknowingly, my mother had indoctrinated me to the victim mentality at the age of 6. It became habit to blame others for my misfortune in life without any self-awareness, laying the foundation for my downward slide from human excellence to the world of never-beens.

So much for my house being a safe sanctuary from school. The street I lived on was made of up of lower to middle class. The street just north of us were lined with low income housing. Many of the kids from this area sold drugs, used drugs, and grew up in problematic households.

To the west of us were the upper class homes built along a manmade lake. They were the doctors, lawyers, and professionals. I was the Chinese kid who couldn't afford nice clothes living in a pre-dominantly Caucasian area. I remember constantly staring at the homes wondering what it would take to live there. Questioning why we were struggling while their kids enjoyed the privileged life. Was it fate? Are we just not lucky enough to be born into money?

With my home life going down the tubes, my school life quickly went south along with it. I was struggling with my grades and language issues. I had absolutely no clue what was going on. All I remember were a lot of x marks on my assignments. One girl who sat beside me was acing all the tests making me feel inadequate.

When the end of the day arrived that was the "real treat." Now I had to walk home and face the school bullies who felt it was cool to pick on the skinny Chinese kid. I don't know what it was but at the time every boy seemed to tower over me. I was so scared of being hurt but what hurt the most was not the physical. It was the degradation of my Chinese heritage, the feeling of not being accepted nor treated as an equal amongst others. Overtime this feeling of inadequacy contributed to my lack of motivation to achieve personal greatness. I didn't believe I could accomplish amazing things because who would want to accept a Chinese guy. At least that was what I was led believe. This self-limiting belief haunted me for many years well into my adulthood.

The next few years the difficulties at home and school began to swing out of control. In 1979, I was playing outside of my house when I heard a tense conversation between my parents and aunt Susan. They were conversing in Cantonese so I only understood bits and pieces of it. I was already in grade 5 and had lost my Cantonese dialect skills as I became more immersed in the English language. It's interesting to note that during this time I began to resent being Chinese. I did everything I could to disassociate myself from the culture much to the disappointment of my parents. I wanted to become more Western so I could be accepted, liked, and respected by others. What was I thinking is what I say today, but I will discuss this concept of confidence in a later chapter.

But back to 1979. After listening closely to the tone of my parent's conversation with my aunt, I went into the house to investigate. As I entered the house before I had the chance to remove my shoes, my father walked across the living room and collapsed in his chair burying his hands in his face, weeping uncontrollably. The years of financial turmoil had caught up with him, forcing him to declare bankruptcy.

The situation called for family meetings on how to proceed. My mom was preparing us to relocate as it looked like our house was going be foreclosed. Bill collectors were coming to take whatever they could to pay off outstanding debts. It was a humiliating experience for my parents who lost face in the Chinese community, a tremendous loss of respect and dignity.

It was embarrassing for myself and my siblings who had to go to school and be subjected to questions on why the tow truck was taking away my family's only car.

We were lucky to be able to keep the family home after the bankruptcy proceedings were completed. To make ends meet, my father worked as a delivery driver for Kentucky Fried Chicken in the most crime ridden area of the city. He worked long hours, yet despite losing his business he still had his entrepreneurial drive. Delivery drivers were paid in two ways, by the hour or by the hour plus payment for each delivery made, including tips.

Almost all of the drivers where happy to collect an hourly wage so they would gladly give my father their deliveries. To them it was easy money, let him take the deliveries to make the extra coin while they sit back in the restaurant to read the newspaper.

My father had a grand plan and that was to plot his comeback in the business world. So far up to this point his business ventures had failed. Every night when he cashed out from his delivery job, he would hand his earnings to my mother and she would take care of the financials.

Times were tough. I remember many instances where the gas company would cut off the supply to our house. My mother would boil water on the stove to add to our bath water just so my siblings and I had a warm bath before heading to bed. There were times when I opened the fridge only to see a few items sitting on the top shelf.

Slowly my parents squirreled away enough money to start a new business venture. In 1980, my parents came home with a plastic vinegar bottle, sawed it in half and spread mung beans on the bottom layer. After a few days of watering, they produced their first batch of bean sprouts. This would be their foray into the produce business.

Starting a business is easy; maintaining and figuring how to make money from it was the hard part. To save on labor, my parents put me and my siblings to work. The hours were long, the work was laborious, and difficult.

There would be no time for a 10-year-old to play. We all had to sacrifice for the good of the family unit.

Year after year, we continued to struggle financially. By the time I became 14, I became increasingly temperamental, resentful, and angry at the world around me. The daily arguments between my father and mom now included me. I grew to resent my parents for putting us into this predicament. What kind of life is this I asked myself? Why have kids if you cannot support or take care of them?

By this time, I stopped caring about what happened at school and home. I dreamed relentlessly about escaping, leaving home and never coming back. That day came in 1993 shortly after I graduated from university when I told my parents I was moving to Vancouver. Their response was no, you are not allowed to go. I screamed back telling them who do you think you are? I'm 23 years old! I did everything you told me to do! I put in my time, finished my studies! What are you going to do, keep me under lock and key forever! I'm outta here tomorrow!

The next day, I waved goodbye to my mom before heading for the departure area at the airport in Winnipeg. When I turned towards the gate it was the best feeling I've ever had. It was like getting out of prison after serving a life sentence. Finally, I told myself! I can now live my life according to my own terms! I can do what makes me happy, engage in the activities I enjoy, and be true to myself!

I was smiling ear to ear especially when I saw the beautiful snowcapped mountains as I flew over British Columbia. That day was the beginning of living for me. For once in my life I felt whole, at peace with myself.

My journey of self-discovery extended beyond enjoying my new hometown. A few months later, my brother Eleazar called me to ask if I've seen something called the Ultimate Fighting Championship. I said "no, what is that"? He replied that it was an awesome martial tournament featuring practitioners from all styles. Kung Fu, kickboxing, judo, wrestling, boxing, sumo, savate, you name it! I immediately headed to the local video store to rent UFC 1. At the time nobody held these types of tournaments, not in the public eye at least. So this idea of mixed martial arts competition was brand new.

After watching it I was amazed at the ferocity of the combatants but what captured my attention the most was a skinny Brazilian named Royce Gracie. Here was this normal looking individual representing the art of Gracie Jiu-jitsu easily beating opponents who were twice as big as him.

Being a skinny guy myself, I saw what was possible for the smaller person. He inspired hope for many and I'm sure many other little people out there as well. That day I took a long look at myself in the mirror asking the questions:

Are you happy with your life?

Are you going to stop blaming your parents for your current life because they are no longer living with you anymore?

What are you going to finally do about it?

I decided that it was time for permanent change in the way I see, and feel about myself. I was tired of feeling angry, tired of feeling sorry for myself, and tired of complaining about why life owes me more.

I began to read personal development books and fitness magazines. I started to workout at the gym to improve my physique, health, and mental outlook. At the time, I couldn't afford Brazilian jiu-jitsu lessons so I stuck to bodybuilding.

In 2004, I enrolled in my first Brazilian Jiu-jitsu class and was instantly hooked. I found myself immersed in the art often studying it until the wee hours of the morning 7 days a week, winning international tournaments along the way.

Today, I'm a proud to hold the honor of black belt, spending my time helping others achieve their highest potential in life. Achieving my black belt has also given me a more reflective vantage point, looking back at my past and from a different perspective.

My parents who I butted heads with for many years, who struggled for so long financially, are now in a great place in their lives. The business that started out of the tiny basement of our home is now located in a big warehouse generating millions in revenue per year.

Being older now we understand each other, and love each other like a real family should. All the negative feelings and ill will is in the past. We've learned from it, deciding it's best to look to the future.

I couldn't have been happier at the way things turned out. My family's struggle had a happy ending after all. I've read lots of comeback stories but I have to say this was probably one of the best comeback stories I have heard in my lifetime. And I'm so proud to have been a part of it.

Why I Wrote This Book

It was Christmas Day on 2013 when I came across a newspaper article in the Vancouver Sun about a Breakfast for Kids program at the local elementary school. The program provides food for children from low income families. They were constantly looking for additional sources to keep up with the growing demand.

As I read the story it brought back a well of emotions inside me, remembering the times when I didn't have much as a child. It was only fitting that I read that article on Christmas Day. It seemed like yesterday I was wishing for that special Christmas gift that never came. So many of those years my greatest joy was going to my friend's house so I could play with their new toys.

I'm always reminded of this feeling when I see my little nieces open their gifts on Christmas day, the joy on their faces warms my heart. During this time, I was running my own fitness business and felt I could make a greater impact in the world. I thought why not help this program as it resonates with my core values and childhood experience. Why not provide joy, hope and promise to kids with very little or nothing in their life?

I connected with the principal of the school and a week later I was in her office discussing how I could use my business to help. I began organizing self-defense seminars to raise food and donations for the program. I also reached out to my clients, asking them to help contribute to the cause.

Collectively, these contributions were a success, and a year later the principal informed me they saw a significant improvement in the children's grades. What was the most rewarding feeling was coming in to personally cook and serve breakfast for the kids. The respect and the appreciation they showed was heartwarming. While there were kids who smiled ear to ear, there were others who had a tired, lifeless expression. I've seen that look before, it was the look I had when I was their age: hopeless, defeated, and sad.

I wanted to go to those kids to give them a big hug, let them know everything will be okay if they are willing to work hard and believe in themselves.

Three years after my initial involvement with the program, the principal of the school contacted to me for a meeting. I thought perhaps she was running short on supplies for the Breakfast Program for Kids. When I arrived at her office, two teachers were present. As the meeting adjourned they explained to me the challenges they had with their programs separate from the breakfast program. One didn't have enough funds to run their spring break soccer program while the other wanted to implement a school robotics program. The robotics program required funding of $10,000 which the school did not have. The principal didn't know how to remedy a solution for this funding shortfall which is why she contacted me.

My efforts in raising funds for the breakfast program was mainly done through my business on a community level. This was enough to make a difference for the lives of the children, but it wasn't enough to create a legacy program that would live on once I was no longer here.

Being in the classroom with these children reminded me of how hope, confidence, and a sense of belonging can be powerful motivators in changing one's situation in life. I could point to my own family situation as a clear example of perseverance and resilience. By harnessing my experiences as an author, martial arts champion, speaker and coach, I could make a greater difference.

For many years, I blamed my parents for our hardship and for my problems. Yes, my parents made many mistakes and they were by no means perfect. But I understand now they did the very best they could with what they had. Neither my siblings and I ran afoul of the law or remained estranged from the family.

In fact, if I could go back in time I would be a better son. Instead of adding to the problems I should have spent more effort in helping with a solution.

Understand that no parent aspires to be a bad one. They don't have kids one day and say I want to mess up this kid's life badly. Sometimes they are left to face circumstances they don't know how to deal with. Like many, they default to the way they were parented. Often it's not the best way, leading many to repeat the vicious cycle over again for the next generation.

It is only when we become self-aware that the vicious cycle is forever broken. A new way of thinking and doing things replacing old negative habits passed on from generation to generation. It is here where we learn the mistakes of the past, replacing them with new positive habits for change.

I agonized over the title of this book, going through many versions. Finally, I decided on "The Human Excellence Project: Lessons Even Awesome Parents Never Teach." I felt this captured the essence of my message to the world. As I mentioned earlier, my parents were not perfect and my upbringing was less than ideal, but my parents gave me many gifts: life, empathy, purpose, focus, discipline, respect for others, and mental toughness. They were awesome parents who prepared me for life in an unfair world. They prepared me for disappointments and setbacks in life, but they never let me give up.

As awesome as my parents and your parents were, there are many life lessons that were overlooked. Not every parent can be everything. We are taught a set rigid curriculum in school. However, I believe if we were taught self-development principles at a young age, we could contribute more to society and to the world as a whole.

The principles I am about to share with you in this book arise from my life experience as a child, as a martial arts master, as a competitive athlete and as an entrepreneur. With the many distractions in the new A.D.D. age, I purposely wrote a book that is easy to read, to the point, and short enough to read in a day. This format will at least I hope, encourage people to begin their journey to personal excellence.

It will force you to shift the way you view your world and all the things around you, making it a more positive one. Each of the principles I share in the book is centered around creating the greatest version of you. In turn, you can help others around you be their very best by sharing what you have learned. Individually and collectively, we can help change the world to think bigger, dream bigger, and achieve things well beyond the status quo. By achieving personal greatness, we can teach others how to develop personal greatness within themselves. It is my mission, our mission, to embark on the Human Excellence Project.

Chapter 1
Patience

A GREAT MARTIAL ARTIST THROUGH years of practice understands that mastery of a technique does not occur overnight. Each level requires new skills, understanding, and continuous practice. Many look for short cuts to achieving success only to be disappointed to realize there is no such thing. Some people buy their way to a black belt status (a "purchased experience"), but they are only fooling themselves. When a master is truly skilled his aura, passion, and knowledge shine through brightly - their confidence, determination, and precision is unmatched.

Success in life, business, and relationships is no different. Patience, persistence, and willpower are all needed to continue forward when life throws a curve ball at us. It is during these times we quickly find out what we are truly made of - are we going to be pretenders or active players in this game of life?

This is the first core principle of my success ideology because I believe before anyone decides they want to be successful, they must first understand it takes time. One has to be mentally prepared to be in for the long haul, and to not give up at the first sign of difficulty. Don't give up because each day you inch closer to your goal, your success, to your next belt level.

Success Is a Marathon Not a Sprint

"Success is the sum of all small efforts, repeated day in & day out"

– R. Colier

When I was 5 years old, my father enrolled me into my first martial arts class at Am Lee Taekwondo. I was living in a pre-dominantly Caucasia area in Winnipeg and I was searching for a hero I could identify with – the hero was Bruce Lee, who passed away two years earlier. Prior to Bruce's rise to fame, Hollywood heroes consisted of John Wayne, James Dean, or Charles Bronson. There was a marked absence of any leading actors who were Chinese.

When my father – who was a master of martial arts himself - took me to see Fists of Fury at a local theatre I was mesmerized by the beauty, power, speed, charisma, and screen presence of Bruce Lee. It was definitely my first "man crush." I wasn't satisfied watching Bruce; I wanted to be Bruce.

The next day, I begged my mom to buy me a Bruce Lee t-shirt at a nearby K-mart store. It was white emblazoned with Bruce in his classic fighting stance along with an intricate dragon design behind him. Oh boy! I really needed it!

With two of my little hands clinging on to my mother's left fingers, I was jumping up and down like a baby kangaroo on six cups of coffee: "Mummy, Mummy, please can I get it?" My mom looked down at me answering with a resounding no, you know we don't have the money for extra things like this.

I looked down to the ground, pursed my lips, and stomped my feet as I returned the shirt to the display table. I can't remember a time when I felt so sad. Bruce was the hero to so many around the world, certainly someone I looked to in times of self-doubt. When we arrived home I pouted the entire day, my mom must have noticed how much the shirt meant to me.

The next day we returned to K-mart, my mom bought a few items she forgot to purchase the day before. Without a word, she reached for the Bruce Lee t-shirt placing it in the shopping cart. "This is for you," she said, turning to me.

As soon as I got home, I quickly put the shirt on. Wow! It's like the power of Bruce took hold of my body to a point I started shake from the excitement.

The next day I proudly wore it to school, who's that on your shirt some of the kids blurted out? It's Bruce Lee the greatest fighter of all time, I proclaimed. Oh really? I've never heard of him. What? You never heard of Bruce Lee?

Where have you been? I guess not everyone shared my enthusiasm for the future legend.

I know one thing for sure. His influence had a profound effect in inspiring me to become a martial artist along with the lessons that came with it.

When my father took me to my first martial arts class, I remember being the only child participant. In the 70's, there were no commercial martial arts kids classes, and being the only kid in the class made me feel uncomfortable. Here I was doing high front kicks with adults towering and sweating all over me. I felt so out of place plus I didn't speak a word of English which made communication difficult. In my mind, I made the decision to not return.

A few days later my father asked me to grab my uniform (a traditional "gi") for class from the closet. I informed him I wasn't going back. He questioned why I wasn't returning, considering I only participated in one class and he had spent all this money on my gi. He had the biggest look of disappointment on his face. It was not the money that mattered but the fact I gave up so quickly. I didn't realize it at the time, but this small incident fostered the beginnings of a limited mindset which I struggled with throughout adulthood. As I got older, I found myself attempting to start martial arts and other activities with enthusiasm but quitting as soon as I felt challenged.

My dad teaching kid's karate class 1970

In 2003, I began my journey into mixed martial arts falling in love with Brazilian Jiu-Jitsu. In my mind I promised myself I would not quit again, committing to daily practice while confronting my fears along the way.

It has been a wonderful journey, taking me from the frail skinny Chinese kid to a championship-caliber martial artist. In 2015, twelve long years of getting my butt kicked I was awarded my black belt in front of my peers, and my father.

My dad is not the type to hug or say he is proud of you. In fact, during the ceremony, he remained stoic, unmoved, serious, and expressionless. Even when I was awarded my black belt, he had the same expression. However, what made me smile the most was a photo capturing him cracking a slight smile out of the corner of his mouth as I gave my thank you speech to the audience. It was almost 42 years ago that I told my father I was never going back to Taekwondo, and now my old man got to see me join him in the highest honor bestowed on a martial artist.

Everything you start in life will have a certain level of discomfort, awkwardness, or a sense of unknown fear. Whether it's starting a new business, activity, or doing something you are not accustomed to, it takes time to get over these feelings.

No one becomes an overnight sensation. We are led to believe people become suddenly rich or successful while not understanding or seeing the hard work or struggle these people endure on their road to greatness.

Receiving my black belt with my dad standing beside me, December 2015.

So many of us give up when the going gets tough for fear we will fail or what others would think of us if we were not successful. Keep in mind, champions and leaders put in the work every day, failing, getting back up, failing again many more times until one day the key to the door unlocks allowing them to see the pot of gold that has been waiting for them on the other side.

Chapter 2
Responsibility

As a martial arts student nears the black belt level, they learn the art of being responsible. They accept accountability for the results that they achieve. Whether they lose a tournament or a make a technical mistake, they do not lay blame on the teacher, the crowd, or events in their life. Maintaining one's emotions and composure is one of the hallmarks of a great martial artist. While an untrained martial artist resorts to anger and violence in a confrontation, the highly trained martial artist will understand they have a choice for their actions. How they respond to the events that occur in their everyday life will determine what they get out of it. If their temper gets the best of them, they have the ability to strike and badly hurt someone, risking assault charges or worse. Or they can choose to walk away without anyone getting hurt. Mental discipline is just as important as physical strength.

Similar to everyday life, how we respond to the events around us largely determines how our life turns out. I do not believe we are 100% responsible for everything in life. Life sometimes puts us in situations by chance. For instance, I would find it hard to believe that a person is responsible for being a passenger in a plane that crashes. However, the practice of accepting responsibility for everything in my life allows my mind to always search for solutions to problems. This is one key point that has transformed my life from one of helplessness to always seeing endless possibilities. Stop blaming others for what you don't have, didn't receive or the lack or results in your life. This will be a giant step in controlling your future success as soon as you grasp this and make this a part of your daily life.

I Was Robbed!

"More people would learn from their mistakes if they weren't so busy denying them."

- Harold J. Smith

In 2012, I was competing at the World Masters Brazilian Jiu-Jitsu championships in Los Angeles. It was a very successful year for me having won a few major tournaments. I had spent months preparing diligently. I was extremely confident that I was going to achieve my goal of being a world champion.

When I got to the arena, I went to the top of the stands to meditate and visualize my upcoming matches. As I slowly entered a meditative state, I kept hearing rumblings from fellow competitors. As I opened my eyes I saw the look of concern around the weigh in stations. One by one each participant was getting disqualified for not making the mandatory weight requirement.

I was so confident I was going to make my weight. I had weighed myself the night before at a local fitness gym and I was 6 lbs. under the weight requirement. No need to worry I had it covered, at least that is what I thought.

It was still early morning the day of my tournament and I wasn't scheduled to fight until late afternoon, so I meandered my way down to the scale at the arena. As I stepped on the scale, I realized that I was 2.5 lbs. over the limit. I frantically ran up the bleachers to inform my teammate Tony Kook that I was overweight. Since he was an Olympic trials competitor in Taekwondo with a vast knowledge in weight cutting, he assured me to not worry and gave me helpful advice on how to get my weight down in time for the crucial weigh-in. He instructed me to grab a garbage bag, punch a hole at the top and wear it like a poncho. Then layer it with my tracksuit and go outside to run laps. As I jogged, he told me to chew gum and spit the saliva out – all of this would help me lose the early morning weight. I went outside to start jogging under the warm rays of the California sun. Beads of sweat starting rolling down my body with every step. About an hour later I re-entered the arena to step on the scale, which now showed I was 4 lbs. underweight. Perfect, I told myself beaming with pride. Now all I had to do was not eat anything and rest up before I was summoned to the ring.

After a long day of waiting, my name was called to the ring. My first opponent was a competitor from New York. As the match started, he came at me aggressively looking to score early. I decided to mitigate his aggressiveness by staying calm to weather the storm while looking to capitalize on his mistake.

Just over a minute into the match he fell for a fake move on my part and I locked on a choke forcing him to tap out. It was a quick victory and gave me a sense that I was not going to lose. I eventually made it to the gold medal round, and I found myself facing a competitor who had won multiple tournaments throughout the year. I was confident he didn't have what it took to beat me that day.

As our match began, I started to attack with a series of techniques that he managed to defend. On a number of occasions, I nearly scored. Usually in this case the referee would award the aggressor what they call advantage points, meaning an almost successfully completed technique. Advantage points come into play if a match ends up tied. The referee would defer to the advantage points to decide the winner.

After four minutes of attacking, it was clear my opponent was not doing anything but stalling and trying to survive. Meanwhile the referee did not award me advantage points despite the various moves I made in almost choking and sweeping my opponent multiple times.

As the match ended, I was elated as I truly believed the gold medal and title of masters world champion was mine. As we were summoned to the center of the ring for the decision, the referee raised my opponent's hand. I lost and was shocked and devastated. The decision was contentious - even my opponent apologized to me stating he was sorry because he didn't want to win that way. My corner was screaming in protest while members of the crowd came down to not only console me but to encourage me to file an official protest. I was numb with disbelief which eventually turned to anger.

I questioned why a referee who is supposed to be impartial would do such a thing. I had trained so hard for this opportunity, only to have an unfair outcome.

When I arrived back in Vancouver, I took my silver medal and placed it in my cabinet. I didn't hang it up on my wall as I wanted it to remind me every day that I was the real champion. For a month I was bitter, refusing to look at video of the match. Whenever someone asked me about it I launched into a big rant of how I was robbed of my first place finish.

Being a personal development coach helped me get through this disappointment. I was self-aware that the bitterness was starting to takeover my daily life. How can I teach people about looking for the good during the bad when I myself didn't? I began to apply the concept of changing how you respond to events in life. You can choose to let life control your mind or you can begin to control it.

In this case, I stopped complaining about what I didn't do or what I should have received. Instead, I focused on what I could do better the next time and accepting responsibility for my loss that day. How would I see it differently? I placed myself in a situation that was in the hands of another person, allowing them to decide my fate. If the referee cheated me from victory is it not his fault because it was not a fair match? I thought to myself perhaps the cards were against me that day but I was at fault for letting the match go to a decision.

Looking back at the match there were times when I could have done more. That's what happens when you leave life up for chance. You may not be happy with your life but how many times are you blaming others for your misfortune and the current state of your life?

We live in a world of complainers, I hate the weather, I wish I had more friends, or I would be more successful if it weren't for this. The list goes on but ask yourself what am I doing to make a significant difference in my life?

How you respond to events in your life is one of the foundations of success. Responding in a positive manner will help you gain new insights on what is needed to drive your goals. So many of us prefer to complain about all the bad things in our life, repeating the same complaints day in day out, often for many years. The question you should be asking is, "what are you going to do about it now?" The game of life throws many curve balls at us. Like a seasoned martial arts master, you must learn how to bend, deflect, and roll with the punches life gives you. To this day, my father credits his martial arts training in helping him transform his failures to huge success in the business world. Many in his shoes would have given up, preferring to make excuses that it was not meant to be. Looking back over the years, I realized he tried many things in business, many of them unsuccessful. In fact, I remember my mom constantly screaming at him for taking so many risks. However, dad always learned and moved on the next day, looking for the right recipe for success until he got it right. His ability to re-focus, and shift in the face of adversity was incredible. I learned a lot from observing my father, his tenacity, work ethic, and relentless pursuit of excellence. With each successful business deal his excitement and positive attitude grew.

Ask yourself how are you responding to the events around you. Taking 100% ownership for your actions will enable you to start producing the success you always dreamed of. Be the pilot, driver, captain, or CEO of your life, steering toward what you want. Positive energy lifts us to the highest level while negative energy makes us unmotivated and less productive. Become the black belt in your career, personal life, and be the shining example for others to follow.

Chapter 3
Passion

ANYONE WHO WANTS TO be highly successful must first discover their passion in life. Many people have defined success as having material goods, whether it is millions of dollars in their bank accounts, a fancy mansion, or being able to afford the finer luxuries in life. While I agree that having money makes life much easier, it is not the sole factor of defining success. I've seen many high level executives make lots of money but feel unfulfilled in their life. In fact, I've seen many of these executives leave their high paying jobs for more meaningful careers, whether that is becoming a snowboard instructor, personal trainer, or baker. One of the best things about having wealth is it provides you with the ability to impact society in a positive way. Socially responsible companies have taken this road such as Tom's shoes which provides services for people in need when someone buys their products.

Having passion gives us purpose and meaning in our lives. It is what gets us excited to get up in the morning, following our dreams, working on them until will we lose track of time not realizing endless hours have passed by. Classic examples of people who are successful but not wealthy are mother Teresa, Martin Luther King Jr., or Nelson Mandela. Their wealth comes from making a difference in the world for future generations.

Many Brazilian Jiu-Jitsu schools barely survive financially. However, the passion of the teachers and owners is so motivating and rewarding to see, particularly in the countless hours they spend teaching, often for free.

Many of the school owners barely break even and squeak out a meager living. However, I witnessed the countless hours they spend teaching many times on their free time. It is truly a great love for them, and the one main theme I hear from all of them is the word "passion." Passion and dedication energizes people and makes them want to continue to pursue excellence.

Take the time to ask yourself what are you meant to do? Are you happy with what you are currently doing? Are you living life according to your own desires and not the desires of others? What do you enjoy doing the most in life?

The things that bring you the most joy are all clues to your life purpose. Start writing them down on a piece of paper and begin aligning your life with this purpose. Not only will you achieve more success but you will be happier.

Knowing Your Why

"Why are you trying so hard to fit it when you were born to stand out"

– Ian Wallace

One of the things that gives me the greatest joy is seeing an individual light up with fire, passion, and enthusiasm for their work. When there is a sparkle in their eye, performing a job they truly love, it's hard not to notice they are truly in touch with what their heart desires.

One of the greatest tragedies in life is regret - when a person utters the words I wish I did this, I wondered if I could have, should have, or done that. Does that sound like you or anyone you know? Don't be ashamed to admit you have these feelings. The majority of the population do get into a rut as they get older. They become set in their ways, creating bad habits, not wanting or knowing how to do things differently.

Often we go through life on auto pilot with all this unlimited potential hiding in each one of us. It's like a treasure chest of gold lost forever in the sea never to be found again.

A number of years ago I watched an interview with Canadian entrepreneur and billionaire Jimmy Pattison. He shared a story about receiving a monthly report on underperforming salesmen at his car dealership. He would call them into his office for a meeting to terminate them. Why not give these salespeople a chance? Jimmy

Pattison has said he was doing a great service for the salesperson because the job most likely wasn't aligned with his gifts or passions. He explained that a great number of the salespeople he terminated thanked him afterwards as they moved on to find jobs in other fields that they found more fulfilling.

I challenge you today to not let your gifts go to waste. Your unique gifts were given to you for a reason, to express yourself fully. Find ways to harness your true passion - there's a world waiting for your help and knowledge. Stop standing on the sidelines and start making an impact.

In Bronnie Ware's best-selling book, The Top Five Regrets of the Dying: A Life Transformed by the Dearly Departing she shared some incredible insights from working with patients in palliative care.

One of the regrets they had was acquiescing to the wishes of others rather than living their life according to their wishes. It was considered one of the most common regrets among the patients. Many of us live our life according to someone else's plan, making them happy but creating misery for ourselves.

In my own experience, I've see this unfold a lot for many Chinese families. Parents have aspirations to want their kids to become doctors, lawyers or professionals whereas trades, arts, or athletics are frowned upon. Perhaps this is felt more acutely in families who immigrate to Canada for a better life. With the opportunities for a better education and livelihood in

Canada, there is often great hope placed on children. Yet, many who do achieve white collar, C-suite executive positions pay a steep price for putting their parents' aspirations above their own passions and dreams.

Death knocking at one's door can force one to re-evaluate how they spent their life, did they accomplish enough in life, was the life something they can be proud of, did they matter or make a significant impact in this world. According to Bronnie Ware, most do not even fulfill half of the dreams they had set out to do.

When I was 26, I realized that my parents controlled most of my life. From the girls I dated, to my career, and my future plans, I had no say in the matter. My life was mapped out for me from the day I was born. At the time I thought my parents were mean spirited, unfeeling, and overbearing.

I came to the conclusion later in life this was not the case. A little over reactive, but not mean spirited. Their intentions actually came from a place of love and of not wanting me to experience some of the hardships they encountered. However, their efforts to protect me kept me in a controlled bubble world, not allowing me to discover things on my own. Their fears soon became my fears, and by the time I reached adulthood I experienced terrible anxiety, low self-esteem, and a limited mindset.

Even when I moved to another city, I still felt like I had to please them. It not only limited my career growth but the ability to formulate decisions based on what I wanted was severely curtailed. While I was miserable, I didn't realize what was actually happening to me, or why I was feeling this way. Then one day the cloud lifted and I decided it was time to make life altering decisions separate from what everyone expected of me. In 2005, I walked away from a secure public sector job with a nice pension to start my own business.

First, I picked up the phone to call my wife to let her know my plans. It was met with anger, calling me crazy for leaving, followed by the slamming of the phone ending the call.

I couldn't blame her for her reaction that day. Most of us have been conditioned from a young age to get a degree, find a stable job, work 40 hours a week, and retire at age 65 with a big fat company pension.

With corporate downsizing, and cutbacks on employee benefits I would have to say this concept of security is an illusion. Recently, I met Bob, a sales business consultant, and former mining executive. He had been employed in the mining industry for many years but was let go after his company downsized. In his late-50s, Bob is too young to retire and considered too old to hire by other companies. He made the decision to continue his career by going into business for himself.

Public sector jobs, once considered the a safe and comfortable career path for people looking for long term stability, has seen its share of cutbacks. One employee I met joked how they may have to start bringing their own water to work now. It's understandable since government spending has come under scrutiny in the decade given the fact many people were out of work after the great recession of 2008.

My decision to leave a corporate job was simple - if you don't control the company, you don't control your destiny. I preferred to be in the driver's seat, navigating where I wanted to go, doing things that resonated with my purpose in life.

That was over 10 years ago, and there has never been a day of regret. It was liberating to spend the next 10 years building a business and achieving my dreams. I made more personal and professional gains during that time than I did the first 37 years of my life. I've met and coached so many interesting people. Meeting everyday people, celebrities, world class athletes, and multimillionaires has allowed me to create a greater life, impact the people I've come into contact with. Starting a business was my opportunity to share my unique gifts with others around the world.

Begin to consider the "why" in your life. What were you meant to do and accomplish in life when you born? What were your dreams growing up? Many of us still have those childhood dreams buried deep inside our soul. They were buried because life got in the way, family, career, or health. Perhaps your parents didn't feel your passion was a real career thereby convincing you to choose an occupation you do not enjoy. Now many years later you have a family to support, a mortgage, and you find yourself counting down the years before you can finally retire. Then you can really start living.

Think back to things that made you truly happy, the activities where you lost track of time. Step out of adult mode for a few minutes, bringing yourself back to your childhood. What did it feel like to engage in that fun activity? Go through it in your mind. Do you feel your emotions suddenly shift? This is your passion begging you to come back. Find a way to nurture it in the present day, rather than waiting too long for action.

Embrace The Winds of Change

"We cannot control the wind but we can direct the sail"

– Thomas S. Monson

I have seen students struggle grasping concepts and techniques at one martial arts dojo only to flourish at another dojo. We often see talented players in sports struggle to become a rising star with one team, yet once traded they suddenly flourish in a new environment under a new coach or system.

During the height of the dot-com craze in the late 1990s, new millionaires were being created at an alarming rate. It seemed like everyone was attempting to get in on the action. Many of my friends were jumping from one company to the next company for better pay. Tech companies were handing out six figure salaries, stock options and a promise of job after graduation. The job fairs were highly competitive, with companies vying for attention from anyone with a tech background. I myself was swept up in the hoopla leaving my accounting job at a major real estate company for a quality assurance position with a software company.

Everything seemed to be on the upswing for a year. Investors were spending money hoping their stock options would make them millionaires. Then in 2000 things started to unravel, and the money began to dry up followed shortly by corporate layoffs in the technology sector.

In my company, we started the year with a few rounds of layoffs. I managed to survive each time until one day I received an email from my manager summoning me to the board room. Like a prisoner on death row I knew the time had come, I accepted as of that day I would join the ranks for the unemployed. It wasn't a big surprise to me as the news of the layoffs was leaked to me by a fellow employee the day before.

As I entered the boardroom my manager informed me my services were no longer needed. I never forgot the looks of the people who lost the jobs that day, some reacted with anger, some shocked, and others devastated. There were a group of computer programmers carrying their belongings in a box, one employee was crying from the entrance of the building to his car. Most of our programmers were from China and were left with an uncertain future.

I chose to look at the experience differently, an opportunity to find something else with more meaning in my life. Up to that point the jobs that I had held in accounting were uninspiring, and I didn't feel they were particularly well suited to my skills. When you are not passionate about what you do, it is difficult to put your best effort in every day. You can get by but you will never be considered an elite performer as it doesn't allow you to use your greatest assets.

The layoff turned out to be an early Christmas present to tell you the truth. I listed the things I didn't like about working there, including having an inept manager who had no people skills. After reviewing the list, it was time to declare my goals, and decide what I truly wanted for my life. It was my big chance to write a new script to my life and set the stage for a new opening and hopefully a memorable ending.

A part of me felt compelled to find another job right away. The influence of my parents still weighed heavily on me, even though I was in my early 30s and hadn't lived under my parents for more than 12 years. My parents valued hard work at all times and staying employed. What would the aunts, uncles, and our friends in the Chinese community think if they found out their oldest son was unemployed?

I was riddled with guilt but knew if I had buckled to their influence I would just be repeating the unhappy cycle all over again. I had to live life for me not for them nor the expectations of what others consider success.

As I sat there on the couch agonizing this decision, a show called The World Deadliest Martial Arts came on. My eyes perked up as they went down the list especially when the military hand to hand combat and mixed martial arts was featured.

It had been a long time since I stepped into a martial arts dojo! I quickly picked up the phone called a local mixed martial arts gym, and the next day I was on the mat training boxing, jiu-jitsu, and kickboxing. For the next six months I didn't work, deciding to live off my savings to train 6 days a week, 4 hours per day, and I loved every waking moment of it.

The experience led me back to my childhood passion long forgotten in pursuit of a career I thought would bring me satisfaction. I was now in the best shape of my life, happy, achieving balance, mental clarity, and self-satisfaction along the way.

I came to realize my true gifts in life were to teach, inspire, and help others less fortunate grow in pursuit of excellence. It provided my life with a deeper sense of purpose and meaning. What is your life purpose? What is your destiny? That is the black belt challenge I'm going to issue you today.

Chapter 4
Awareness

ONE OF THE KEY elements separating a martial arts master from a beginner is the understanding of self-awareness. Through years of relentless practice, they are able to see, feel, hear, subtle changes around them. These skills not only help them shift techniques instinctively based on intuition and touch but it also creates a higher awareness of themselves. The many years of discipline, focus, and meditation creates a highly intuitive human being at the master level, making them natural self-coaches. Their techniques have been honed through the years to make the most efficient economy of movement. Where a beginner may expend too much energy by using force and strength, the master would move effortlessly only using what is necessary to complete the movement while maximizing impact at the same time. The master wastes little time, getting rid of unnecessary movements that do not provide the best route to successful execution.

How does your life compare? Is it full of noise and distractions like a beginner martial artist? Are you using lots of energy and effort but find yourself sinking further down the ladder to success? Take a look around you, what is absorbing all your energy? Unfinished work? A cluttered home or desk? Indecision to make changes?

The less you have to worry about, the more energy you have to focus on the things that will generate the most impact in your life.

Practicing the art of self-awareness allows you to truly understand yourself and the things that make you unique. It allows you to see what areas you are strong in and which ones can use improvement. It is the trademark of great martial artists, leaders, athletes, and world class performers.

Free Up Energy by Decluttering Your Life

"Courage is the power to let go of the familiar"

- Raymond Lindquist

When I was a child going through the financial struggles of my parents, I found myself feeling less focused as the years went by. My grades plummeted by the time I entered high school. A chaotic household was reflected in dropping grades and performance at school. When your life becomes mentally cluttered, it's easy to lose sight in what you believed in.

In the martial arts we often see this pattern in students who train at one school then jump to another school a year later. They exhibit a behavior of studying a variety of martial arts but never stay long enough to be a true expert. Often the student drops out due to personal issues at home. Instead of dropping out, I would encourage these students to continue their practice and use the dojo as a way to de-stress and refocus on a goal.

Many top performers practice some form of mindfulness training such as tai chi, yoga, or meditation. We need quiet time to reflect, clear our mind, and ground ourselves.

Highly focused individuals minimize the physical clutter around them such as a messy house, workstation, or unfinished projects like a half completed basement. Operating in this environment causes stress, it also takes up more mental power as we need to constantly think about it.

Take a moment to think of this scenario, if you have a messy desk. How much time do you spend looking for a document when you need it? Sometimes you cannot find it and you become frustrated. Not only are you not operating at the most efficient level but you stagnate yourself from doing the things necessary for your success.

This goes the same with unfinished projects. How many of you know of people who always say they are busy but never seem to get ahead? They have all these great ideas, attend every personal development seminar course, and start a project but never see it through to completion.

Physical clutter robs us of energy and productivity. The biggest issue for me are old electronics, clothes I no longer wear, newspapers, or old magazines. My wife especially loves to hang on to things for years, items that we no longer use. I have to say it drives me nuts. The general rule for me is if I haven't worn or used the item for a year I toss, recycle or give it away.

Take a few hours to go through your closet, office, or kitchen. See which items you can clear out to make your environment a clutter free zone. You will feel free, confident, and productive.

Be Honest with Yourself

"I think self-awareness is probably the most important thing towards being a champion."

- Billy Jean King, Former World Tennis Champion

My father was my coach at a local martial arts tournament when I was 16. He was not the most patient teacher, demanding excellence and perfect execution. Often he would teach a new technique once or twice and if you didn't perfect it he would grow extremely frustrated. It was reflected in his voice and tone. Only people with thick skin would continue in my father's classes.

That day I was scheduled to compete in the weapons forms division and contact sparring. During the weapons routine I forgot my steps, finishing in third place much to my father's dismay. It got even worse in the sparring portion where I went up against the eventual champion who blew me out of the water. He was extremely strong, and kept nailing me with a sidekick, scoring at will while I tried to defend helplessly. I felt embarrassed and humiliated that day especially with all the friends and family who watched from the bleachers.

As we drove home my father berated me for my performance, telling me I was lucky to even place third in the forms division. My younger brother Eleazar had won his division which made me feel even more ashamed at my performance. When we arrived home, I went to my room angrily tossing my third place trophy into the garbage can.

That night as I laid stewing in my bed, I thought how much I resented my father for treating me in such a manner. Here I was watching my friends from school get pats on their back of encouragement from their parents and all I ever received was harsh criticism. I was criticized for everything from my looks, to my grades, and was being reamed out for being a bad kid. At the time, I was unaware that what I was experiencing in my childhood was quite common in Chinese households. This kind of parenting – it was believed - would toughen kids mentally, keep them in line, prepare them for the real world.

I began to ask myself, "do I really need to do this martial arts?" My love for it was beginning to fade as criticism from my dad mounted. I decided that day I was going to quit instead of trying to live up to my father's expectations. I began to venture into track and field where I excelled as a provincial champion in long jump. It was definitely a great change of scenery as I was under a very encouraging coach for a few years. It seemed as though martial arts would become a distant memory.

It was years later that I realized my interest in martial arts was still buried deep inside of me.

When I left university and moved to Vancouver, I didn't have a lot of money. My new roommate Angelito shared my passion for the martial arts. After seven years of being away from the martial arts, I began practicing with him again in our tiny apartment. We bought punching and kicking pads. Since we didn't have money for TV we passed the time working on our techniques. As I began to rediscover my love for the martial arts, I suddenly saw a shift in my thinking after reading self-help books. I asked myself was I really a terrible martial artist my father made me out to be? Am I really not that good? Or was he just saying that to teach me to find the solutions within myself. The truth was I really wasn't that good, in fact looking back at that time I didn't spend enough time training to be my best. I didn't put in the necessary time and work like the other students, I just did enough to get by.

I then began to think about what if? What if I decided to fully commit to being the best I could be? How would it turn out? What would I accomplish? How far can I possibly go? Growing up I did not take criticism well. I let these words get to me, allowing them to hold me back from reaching my full potential. No one had taught me that criticism is just feedback on what you need to succeed. Instead of taking the advice in stride I took it to heart opting to quit and preferring to move on to something more safe or less demanding.

That day was the turning point in my life. When things don't go according to plan, I sit down to have a conversation with myself. Like a football coach going over a game recap after the team loses, looking for areas for improvement. It is not merely enough just to do a review of your weaknesses but you need to do it as objectively as possible. At times our biases can cloud our judgement forcing us to make the same mistakes over again. A great way I like to counter this is to include a group of advisors or friends who will give me frank feedback while I take down notes.

It is up to me to go over these notes to decide which feedback to use for improvement. This process has transformed me from a shy anxious kid to professional speaker, from mediocre martial arts competitor to a champion, and from a white belt to black belt. I can now look at the world from the perspective of a master.

I've seen adult beginner and intermediate students throw tantrums on the mat, some even running to the washroom to cry or vent when they lose to another classmate. The one advice I always give them is if they want to become great they must first be honest with themselves. This can be difficult for many of them especially the ones who have already won some tournaments and start to develop a superiority complex. No matter how many accolades you win, there is always fear in every successful competitor. The champion knows their own fears and constantly faces those fears until they are conquered. Fake champions want others to believe they don't have fears, they assume what got them to where they are currently will continue to win at the higher levels. This is far from the truth as I've seen people who were great competitors at a blue belt level only to get destroyed at the purple level. For most the defeat is too much to bear, the commitment to facing the truth is too much work so they elect to quit all together. It's sad when I see this as many have the talent to go farther but stop when they are on the cusp of greatness.

Think about how this applies to your life. How many times have you been on the cusp of greatness only to walk away? Did you really take time to look at yourself objectively? Start tearing apart your thoughts, emotions and decisions in all areas of your life, putting them under a microscope. You will gain new insight and clues about why you act a certain way and what changes need to be made.

Take the time to write down these areas that need to change, and indicate what actions you will take to foster change. Have your friends, family and people who care about you provide you with valuable feedback. Think of it as your personal review committee for managing growth. It will give your life clarity, clearing the path for goal attainment leading to excellence and success.

Chapter 5

Respect

PARENTS OFTEN ENROLL THEIR children in martial arts training to learn the core value of respect and loyalty. Teaching the value of honoring your commitments, and helping others succeed as much as you help yourself. It is also about honoring the master and fellow senior students for helping you climb the ranks to black belt.

One of the most valuable lessons I took away from martial arts training was staying committed, and gaining the respect of others around me as a dependable, reliable person. This has taught me to focus on what needs to be done to accomplish a goal while at the same time having the ability to call on the right people to help me get there.

If you are one of those people who are constantly frazzled, late for meetings, or unable to keep your commitments to people, then pay close attention to this chapter.

Make Your Word Gold

"Don't respect someone for making a promise. Respect them for keeping it."

- Susan Gale

While the martial arts code of respect is something everyone should adhere to, not all martial arts students follow this route even when they are close to receiving their black belt. Money and greed usually turn some students and masters into disrespectful people, flying against all the values martial arts stand for.

It is the sole reason why my father James Chan and my Brazilian Jiu-jitsu teacher Todd Nathanson have only handed out less than 6 black belts at the time of this writing. A student must demonstrate these core values over a course of 13 years or longer. Unfortunately, most schools today worry about losing students therefore promote much more quickly without the student showing long term commitment, integrity and loyalty to the master.

I've seen masters who have stood by and helped these students tossed to the curb all in the name of money. I've encountered students who have forgotten the concept that successful people don't get to the top by themselves. They have successful caring people surrounding them. You would think common sense would be applied in situations like this, which is you don't screw people over who've helped you. I'm often left shaking my head, asking where is all the respect this student or black belt should have learned from martial arts. When I was 16 years old, there was a senior black belt student in my class. At the time he was 21 years old and had been training since he was 10 years old. He was brash, cocky, and I noticed he liked to act tough by bullying some of the beginner students. One day during class, the grandmaster demonstrated a technique with him to the class. As they completed the technique, the student was required to bow to the grandmaster as a sign of respect. Instead of bowing, he turned his back defiantly away from the grandmaster and walked away. After a few more incidents, the grandmaster had no choice but to kick him out of the school. The next day one of the oldest students in the class shared a valuable lesson with me. "After all the grandmaster had done for this student over the years, this is how he repays him?" he remarked to me. It is these words that have stuck with me throughout my life.

The martial arts not only teach you respect but staying true to your commitments as well. Very few people in this day and age keep their commitments. They agree to do something and back out later. This does two things: it makes it difficult for you to complete your goals and it makes others lose respect for you as a person. When people don't respect you they will not help you get what you want. You will not have the necessary tools to build your success.

It can also be mentally draining to constantly have this guilt or the drama weighing on your mind, taking away the mental power to focus on driving success.

The martial arts are not all about physical ability. The masters look for how the students interact with their fellow training partners. If students do not like or respect each other, they will quickly find that they have no one to train with. This kind of student will find progress to the highest level a challenge.

This is no different when applied to everyday life. If you gain the reputation as a reliable and dependable friend, employee, or relative, someone will always be willing to go out of their way to help you when the need arises.

I remember a local martial arts instructor I knew, a charismatic guy with the gift of gab. The only problem was his loyalty - he was constantly changing gym locations, teaching at one gym until he wore out his welcome then hopping to the next best thing. To make matter worse, he dragged his students through this merry go round, never providing any real stability. He talked about wanting success but never stayed committed to his plans. In fact, I once referred a client to him that turned out to be a poor experience. The final straw was when the client drove a considerable distance from the suburbs to downtown only to find out there was no class. Nobody had bothered to tell him. The instructor's unreliable reputation quickly spread among the martial arts community as a person not to be trusted, and it didn't take long for this teacher to close up shop and leave town.

Apply these lessons by staying true to your commitments, and stop promising things you cannot deliver. If it means saying no to people in order for you to stick to your promises, then do so. Enter your commitments into a calendar, review them daily to ensure you do not miss or show up late.

Re-examine your life to find out what unfinished business you have lingering. Was there a promise you made but didn't follow through with? Perhaps in your business, career, health or marriage?

In recent years, I've learned to use the power of saying no to things I couldn't commit to. I will speak more about this concept in a later chapter. Too often we worry about what others will think of us if we don't agree to a commitment. It is in situations such as these we get into trouble and begin to feel overwhelmed and stressed. Start living life for yourself before making others happy because you can only make others happy when you are happy.

Manage your time wisely, respect your time and others. When you are seen as dependable by others, you will trust in yourself to follow through with your personal commitments to success, more money, better health, and fostering great relationships. Always remember and acknowledge the people who have helped you along the way.

Chapter 6
Focus

A HIGHLY SKILLED MARTIAL arts master is able to pinpoint the exact spot to hit a brick, smashing it into bits while the unskilled would break their hand. It can take many hours to master and channel one's energy to one specific area.

Like the master, you too can apply the art of focus to what you want to accomplish in life. When one is focused, there is nothing anyone can do to stop them from moving towards their goal. Every champion has a high level of focus. They write down what they want and their brain goes about bringing all the necessities together to accomplish that goal.

Maintaining focus is hard to do in today's world, where we are bombarded by social media, information from our smartphones, and 24/7 news all day long. We have so many more distractions now more than ever before. When I was growing up Coke, Pepsi, 7-Up, and Sprite were the mainstream choices for soft drinks. Now we have massive shelves of drinks to choose from such as bottled water, flavored water, different types of cola, you name it. It's no wonder we live in an attention deficit age where focus amongst teens is almost non-existent.

I want you to be the martial arts master, and shut out all the noise around you. Begin to focus on the one goal that will get you to your destination. Easier said than done in today's world. So how should you go about this?

Like the Shaolin monks, one needs to get away to some place tranquil to quiet the mind. In other words, create a system in your environment to minimize the distractions around you. Begin focusing on all the good in your life regardless of the circumstances, channel all your energy into what you want out of life. Ask yourself what does my heart want me to do?

I Want You!

"Stop saying I wish, start saying I will"

– David Copperfield

The first Rocky movie was one of the most memorable feel good movies ever made. There was good reason to why it won so many awards inspiring many generations. Everyone loves the story of an underdog who manages to beat the odds, forever changing their fortunes.

One of the scenes I will never forget is the one when Rocky's opponent Apollo Creed makes his entrance to the ring repeatedly chanting, "I want you!" This is a classic form of intimidation and showmanship, psyching out one's opponent.

Although Rocky was a movie, Apollo as a champion did what all successful people do - declare what they want. They don't have time to be wishy-washy or indecisive. Their mind is made up on what their intentions are, all the plans are laid out on how to achieve it, and it is then executed masterfully with the highest precision.

While a few don't require the motivation to follow through with their goals, the majority wander aimlessly through life. They don't think about tomorrow let alone the next decade. Like hiking across the jungle without a GPS, they become lost, disoriented, or perhaps killed by predators. They may eventually get to their destination; but most won't as the jungle is an unforgiving environment.

A skilled hiker, on the other hand, always embark on their journey with an intention, knowing the potential dangers ahead they carefully plan out the safest most efficient route to get to their destination.

So many of us wander through life like a lost hiker, leaving our success in life to chance rather than taking control of our own journey. To become your best, you must first declare what you want.

When I was contemplating competing at the international level in Brazilian Jiu-jitsu many years ago, I was very apprehensive. I had competed in two local tournaments, but wasn't confident I could be successful in the events that brought competitors from around the world.

Unsure of myself or not, I declared out loud in my office one day, "I'm going to go compete at the Las Vegas Open in 2010, and I'm going to win gold!" As soon as I declared my goal I set the action plan in motion. First, I Googled all the winners in all the major tournaments that year, looking for patterns. One guy named Brian caught my attention as he was winning all the big tournaments. I figured I would find out as much information as I could on this competitor since it was most likely we would face each other in the finals if I made it to the gold medal round. Four months leading up to the tournament I studied his matches on YouTube. He was a very strong powerful athlete with legs the size of tree trunks, and usually overwhelming opponents with his aggressiveness in the tournaments.

This was the perfect opponent for me as my game relied on trickery, misdirection, and countering one's aggression.

On at a hot summer August day in 2010, we met in the finals, and true to the research I had conducted, he came at me in his usual aggressive style. I quickly tied him up to slow down the pace. I could feel he was uncomfortable in this position, wanting to set up a trap I pushed into him on purpose to get him to aggressively push back. That was all I needed as I sent him soaring through the air on to his back. He frantically tried to get back on top but I was all over him, and within a few seconds I administered a choke forcing him to tap out at 1:30 seconds into the match. The referee raised my hand and as I turned to the crowd I felt so proud to be a champion that day. It was not the gold medal that mattered to me, but the feeling of pride knowing I had declared my intention, flawlessly executed it, leading to victory on the podium that day.

If you want to be your best, make sure you declare your intentions, create an action plan on how to achieve it, focus, and execute. In time, you will stand among the elite, as a proud champion and a leader.

Always Be Grateful for the Life You've Created

"Be grateful for the things and people you have in your life. Things you take for granted someone else is praying for."

- Marlan Rico Lee, Musician

In 2016, we witnessed the mass exodus of Syrian refugees fleeing their war torn home country in massive numbers. Entire families left everything behind with only the clothes on the back, crossing into international waters on makeshift boats. Some died as they attempted to make it to a refugee camp in a nearby country. One of the haunting images shown on news agencies around the world was the dead body of a 3-year-old boy named Ayan Kurdi lying face down on a beach in Turkey. His family's boat capsized when they encountered rough seas, taking the lives of both his mother and brother, leaving his father as the only survivor. Hearing these kinds of stories make me sad but at the same time proud of the country I live in. We have a right to education, freedom to express ourselves, and endless opportunities to get ahead.

Too often I hear citizens complain about the country we live in - the weather, the taxes - believing they are entitled to something they don't reserve.

So many of these stories make me want to give these people a good shake. I remember a story of a friend's brother-in-law. This guy was treated so well by his in-laws, often inviting him over for dinner whenever he was free. All he would do was complain about the food, frequently remarking "I can't believe we are eating this again". I can't believe this guy would be so disrespectful. I remember not having much to eat growing up, so I always welcome a free home cooked meal. No matter how successful I become I constantly remind myself how many people out there in the world would trade places with me in a heartbeat.

My father and mother used to tell stories of their childhood, fleeing their village when the Japanese started bombing. I have friends who were a part of the Vietnamese boat people who fled after their country fell to the communist. Every year they still show their appreciation to Canada by helping serve meals at the local soup kitchen.

I have many immigrant friends; some are still working towards success but no matter how difficult their challenges are; they always flash that smile of appreciation for living in a great country.

In the book, Man's Search for Meaning, holocaust survivor Victor Frankl found that those who survived in the concentration camps the longest were not the physically strong but the ones who managed their attitude and environment. From this experience he believed our drive in life is not power nor pleasure but finding things that have meaning in our lives. By having meaning, individuals can survive even the most challenging conditions.

To find meaning in our lives, Frankl believes this can be achieved by:

1. Interacting authentically with people and the environment around them.

2. Giving back to the world around them.

3. Changing how we view things that are out of our control. For example, losing the ability to walk after a major stroke.

We can have everything taken from us but one thing that cannot be taken is our attitude. Picture yourself three to five years from now. Where would you like be? How much money would you like to have in the bank account? What would be your contribution to society? Will you be enjoying life with the special someone you've always dreamed about? Will you be healthy?

If you are one of those women who say all guys are scum, then you will most likely going to attract more of those in your life. If you believe you will always struggle with money, then you will always have financial worries. Start celebrating all the things you do have; it could simple as having the ability to get up in the morning and enjoy a walk down the street.

Learning to appreciate everything life offers us is key to developing our ability to manifest our positive energy. One of the daily tasks we can do to help us fulfill our desires is to create a gratitude list. So what is a gratitude list and how does one go about creating one?

Gratitude lists or a gratitude journal are basically lists of things we are thankful for in life. Creating a gratitude list is a great way to reprogram our minds especially if we want to rid negative thoughts.

Some experts recommend writing out ten to fifteen things you are grateful for daily. In my opinion, this can be quite a bit to take on if you are just starting out. Especially if things in your life are not going as well as you would like. In this situation it could be difficult to find things to be positive about.

I recommend writing down just three to five until you get more comfortable. This can be compared to starting a new exercise program or diet. If I just told you to go full steam ahead and do a complete 180-degree lifestyle change you might be motivated the first week or so, but then you will soon quit as the goal seems unreachable. Therefore, it's important for the goal to be measurable and achievable when starting out. If you have more than five then great, write as many as you can think of.

The main thing here is to remain consistent and do it every day. You can use a notebook or any other format that you prefer. I like to use a gratitude list template which I print out and organize in a report folder. I then place it on the night stand beside my bed.

Write about all the things you are grateful for in life. Even if your life isn't where you want it to be at the moment there are always some positives.

For example, you can be grateful for having enough to eat, a place to sleep, lots of great friends who care about you, or just living in general.

You can even take that a little deeper. I like to look up at the trees and all the things around me. I appreciate how nice it is to be living in such a beautiful city. I notice the greenery, the fresh air, and am thankful for being healthy. As I do this I begin to feel the positive energy flow through my body.

I have to admit this took some time to sink in. When I first started a gratitude list I must have sat there for 30 minutes thinking this will never work. As I opened up my heart and my feelings, things began to flow.

In the past, I could never see the good things in front of me. It seemed like those things were always for other people.

However, this process has allowed me to see opportunities where I used to only see problems.

It changed my thinking pattern to look at each situation not as a problem but question what is the situation telling me. I normally would have a solution within minutes. In the past, I would stew and grieve about the problem. Now I look at it as a challenge to learn and further myself, bringing me closer to my goals. If I can do this, so can you!

I'm not any more special than you nor is a celebrity. We all wake up in the morning and put our pants on the same way. One leg at a time.

Some experts suggest writing your gratitude journal in the morning as it will put you in a positive mood before you start your day. I prefer to do mine in my bed right before I go to sleep.

I believe this is important and this is my theory. I want the last thing on my mind before I go to sleep to be positive. That way when I sleep I dream only positive images. This method has not failed me.

Remember the main thing is to stick with it and consistently do it every day. The main point of journaling your positive thoughts is it helps heighten your recognition of positive things. This will help you live in the moment which is what matters the most.

Too often we get frustrated over what we want and don't presently have. Instead, what we should be focusing on is the little positive things that happen to us each day and learn to appreciate them.

As you practice this more you will notice a shift in your thinking pattern. You will slowly begin to see that there are many positive things in your life. This will enable to your mind to come up with multiple options to enable you to attract what you desire.

If you've never practiced this before it might seem a little weird and you may not believe it. However, I can honestly say from my experience it does work. In cases where I used to see no opportunity in a business idea, I now see opportunities everywhere. It forces you to use your creative mind like you never did before.

Once again take action starting today. I know you won't regret your decision!

Focus on Enjoying Life's Beautiful Moments

"Slow down and enjoy the journey right now. Take time for the people in your life. They won't always be there."

Joel Osteen – American Preacher

I had a cousin named Edmond who was bright, easy going, and ambitious. When he was 1 years old his father, my father's oldest brother Uncle Johnny, passed away. Edmond's mom decided to start a new life in another city across the country.

It would be 22 years before I got to see him again. I was so happy to finally connect with him after all these years. All the memories I had of him over the years were through family photo albums. I had always wondered what he was doing, what he was like? He had a quirky sense of humor and loved his sports.

Growing up without a father was tough. His mother supported him and his sister working at a low wage job at a sewing factory while living in social housing. Despite not having an economic advantage, Edmond diligently put himself through university, graduating with a degree in business. Shortly after he landed a job with a major financial institution where he quickly rose through the ranks. Life was getting good. He saved enough money to buy his own condo, and even had enough to help provide his sister with a down payment for her place.

I couldn't have been happier for him after all the struggles he had been through. On top of this success, he began seriously dating a new girl. They travelled to South America spending time to enjoy life. It was to my delight when he informed me one day that he had proposed to her.

As the months rolled by, my wife began to ask why we hadn't received a wedding invitation. I reassured her that everything was fine and she was worrying about nothing. Months continued to go by and we didn't hear anything about the wedding.

I grew increasingly concerned. Did they break up? Then I received a call from Edmond one day and he informed me that he had been diagnosed with pancreatic cancer. I was shocked and devastated. Cancer did not run in our family. I was angry - why did this have to happen to Edmond after all the hard work he put in to build a great life for himself and his future wife. There are so many people out in the world creating evil, and here was a guy who was creating good. Why him?

The prognosis for recovery was not good. Pancreatic cancer does not have a high rate of success when it comes to a cure. Despite knowing this, my cousin fought everyday while putting up a positive outlook. He did not want the others around him to cry, and kept us smiling despite experiencing unbearable pain.

In the fall of that year he passed away, and I flew to Toronto to pay my respects along with other members of my family. The experience of losing a cousin close to my age had a profound effect on how I would live the rest of my life. As I sat on the plane ride back to Vancouver, I thought about my life. What lesson can I learn from this? How can I make things better for myself and the people around me so when the day comes to meet my maker I will have lived it fully without regrets?

Too often many of us live life on auto pilot, going through life without thinking or trying to accomplish new things to enrich ourselves, to make ourselves happy, or cherish what we have around us. We continue on this long road trip without stopping to admire the sights along the way. Then one day we are lying on our death bed, wishing we could have done things differently, or had just taken the opportunity to enjoy things more when we had the chance.

Edmond's passing pushed me to go beyond my comfort zone. I started to learn how to get over my fear of public speaking, to use my voice to spread my message to the world, to think bigger instead of hiding in the comfort of mediocrity. Most importantly it taught me to love more, forgive more, and to appreciate every little thing life has given me.

I was really pleased that Edmond had the opportunity to travel extensively around the world with his fiancé before his passing and had those memories with her. Take time to savor these moments, the time with your family, to volunteer to help a charity or cause, or to make a commitment to travel to places you never been.

We all believe time is infinite by saying don't worry about this, or that can be done tomorrow, but we never stop to ask ourselves what if tomorrow never comes. Give your loved ones a hug, compliment someone, and accept compliments back with gratitude. We have one life to make it right, make it a work of art, make it worth remembering.

Chapter 7
Discipline

ONE OF THE MOST important questions I ask myself every day before I go to sleep at night, is what do I need to do make my dreams a reality. What do I need to dedicate fully every day to help me reach that ultimate goal? Too many of us wish for things but like a car without gas, it sits in the driveway day after day, being immobile and inert. It's time to fill that tank, rev the car engine, and proceed to your intended destination.

What makes the martial arts a great tool for teaching goal setting and commitment is the belt ranking system. A student learns which techniques and expectations are required to reach each belt level. When one set of challenges are met, they receive a new belt which provides them with greater confidence and skill. Each level becomes more difficult to attain thereby pushing the student beyond what they are comfortable with.

Like the belting system, create an outline of your goals on paper. Spend time writing them down, constantly reviewing on a daily basis. Your brain will begin to engrain these goals into your subconscious mind along with all the things you will need to achieve it.

Beating The Odds

Successful people do what unsuccessful people are not willing to do. Don't wish it were easier, wish you were better.

- Jim Rohn

When I work with extremely successful clients, ones who have become self-made multi-millionaires, everything seems easy to them. A deal here and a deal there, and like magic the never ending flow of money comes gushing out like a beautiful waterfall. I always ask them two questions, how did they start, and what motivates them to keep going long after they have made their fortune? I have yet to have met anyone in my life that was born into wealth, although I am sure they are out there. Coming from nothing myself, I love the underdog story of triumphing over the odds. There are two individuals who come to my mind when this subject of financial success comes up: Steven L and Scott Piccott, both whom made their fortune in real estate.

Steven grew up in a working class family on the east side of Vancouver, and began his journey into the world of real estate development when he bypassed university to work as a waiter. While working at the restaurant, he teamed up with two other waiters to buy their first house. It was a brilliant move as he began to leverage (or "flip") the house into more properties over the years. Today, he has a multi-million-dollar portfolio of real estate developments. Many of the condo projects in and around the Vancouver downtown area are due to his involvement.

What I admire most about Steven is he is still very down to earth, driving an older Toyota Camry around town. I remember once asking him if he ever worries about losing it all? He responded that he never thinks about that, "you can't", he added. In fact, he stated he had almost lost everything not that long ago, but his focus was always on what he would gain as a reward for succeeding, and not wasting energy on thinking about the penalty if he should fail.

Steven's approach is no different than the mindset of a black belt champion, who sacrifices hard training, possible long-term injury, and time away from family or the chance of winning the big prize. Steven's advice is to always look at the positives involved, the potential gain of moving forward towards goals, and what would be lost due to fear? Most people have this play it safe mentality and are not willing to think of new ways to better themselves, opting instead to complain about why life in unfair.

My other friend Scott Piccott, author of The Unlikely Millionaire, had an even more compelling rags to riches story. Born with a learning disability, he quickly fell behind his classmates when he was young. He had a reading level of a grade 5 student by the time he reached high school. Counselors began recommending he become a tradesperson as it seemed like any hope of attending university seemed out of reach. His mother, a school teacher, never gave up on him, spending countless hours tutoring him, helping him read, and most importantly providing him with a positive nurturing environment. What I also found amazing is Scott came from a single family home where finances were tight every month. Night after night his mother encouraged him to continue to be his best, to not let this disability stop him from doing great things in life.

With his mother's belief in him, Scott not only graduated high school but college as well with a Diploma in Management. Shortly afterwards he moved to Calgary to work for Air Canada. Like many wide eyed college graduates he welcomed the opportunity it gave him, perhaps a long career in the corporate world. Not long after starting his new job he was laid off. Faced with the prospect of not having a steady income he took on a security job spending hours watching a door open and close. To alleviate the boredom, he began reading self-help books, and one that caught his interest was "Rich Dad Poor Dad" by Robert Kiyosaki. It was this book that gave Scott the idea of taking control of his personal life instead of having someone else call the shots for him. After a year on the job, he saved up enough to put a down payment on a house which he rented out. Now a landlord, he began to study the real estate market accumulating three houses in less than a year. In a savvy maneuver, he then traded his start up homes for an apartment building which he redeveloped. When the apartment was back on the market for re-sale, he sold all the units in less than a day catapulting him to the leagues of the multi-millionaires.

One day I sat down with Scott for lunch and asked him what are some of the key things he used to build his successful real estate empire. Other than lots of reading on successful people, he spent many hours visualizing. One of the stories he shared with me was if he saw a building he wanted to buy he would sit in front of the building staring at it, visualizing what it would be like once he owned it. He then would think about the current owner, what was their mindset? Did they have a cash flow problem, were they tired of managing the property? He then thought about how he could make it a win-win situation for himself and the owner. It was never about how much he could get, but to ensure he could offer a solution or be an ally to the owner. In most cases he told me this has worked very well for him in his dealings.

It is said that a positive thought is twice as strong as a negative thought. This is all so true as I have never seen a martial arts competitor become a winner by constantly thinking otherwise. In fact, if you say you will never win, this will likely be the outcome. It's no wonder why so many people who grow up in impoverished neighborhoods never leave, continuing to get sucked into a never ending cycle of poverty, crime, and drugs. The environment reinforces their belief into thinking they can never better their circumstance, telling their subconscious mind they will always be poor, nothing more. As a result, the limited thinking becomes engrained in their collective consciousness, and passed on to future generations.

However, despite the widespread poverty in these areas there are always stories of the one individual who defies the odds, going on to college, or building a successful career. This takes place despite of their surroundings, whether it be seeing their family members struggle financially, dropping out of school, dying from a drug overdose or drive by shooting.

Why does this happen? Like my two friends, Steven and Scott, these individuals adopted a world class mindset, a black belt mentality to forge on despite set-backs. They ignored the naysayers and did what others were not willing to do. In martial arts, this could be sacrificing your body to get to the next level. In business, it could be getting up 5am in the morning to be the first one in the office and leaving at 10pm as the last person to turn off the lights. It could mean cleaning toilets at a local McDonalds as a new immigrant, setting aside your pride because you were a doctor in your old country. If you want to be the best, you need to ask yourself what kind of sacrifices are you willing to make, not just a half-heartedly, but on a daily basis without the guarantee of success. Are you willing to forget about failures, concentrating on the moment, leaving the disappointments behind?

If success is what you want, prepare yourself mentally by taking these questions into account. In my martial arts career, the students who are able to mentally block out their past failures make the biggest gains towards greatness.

Chapter 8
Confidence

Last week a stranger slowly walked into the dojo to inquire about classes just when I was finishing up teaching a class. It's quite common to see shy people unsure of themselves coming in to check out whether or not martial arts is for them. Some are curious, others are enthusiastic, but most in general are quite nervous to be walking into a new environment. Just seeing all the people sweating away, hitting the punching bags, along with people being tossed in the air on to the mats can be intimidating for a newbie. With some encouragement, and easing of their concerns the majority – like this stranger - sign up for a free trial. A few months later I often get the response, "I can't believe how this has changed my life, I wish I had done this sooner!"

Many people put off their dreams because they don't know how things will turn out. It is that uncertainty that causes them to not try in the first place. I remember as a kid I refused to eat certain Chinese delicacies like chicken feet. My parents used to get upset and say, "how do you know you do not like it if you never tried?" Those words rang hollow then but it couldn't be more true today for me.

Trying out your first martial arts class can be apprehensive but after a few classes the feeling quickly dissipates. So many of us live life leaving opportunities on the table because of our reluctance to attempt something new. Some of my best discoveries about myself have come from trying new things way out of my comfort zone. Not everything I tried has worked for me or made me a raving fan, but each time I delved deeper into learning more about myself as a person. It taught me to be open for change to bring possibilities that I may have overlooked.

The main point is you need to just *start*. If it means writing a new book, don't worry about making it into a masterpiece. Start writing it, clear the negative thoughts from your mind, and let the words flow. Before you know it you will have completed your first book.

Start today moving the needle forward, and building the necessary momentum. The goal may seem far away at first, but like that car heading towards your vacation destination, you will eventually see it in horizon from your window. It is then you will realize it's only a matter of time before you arrive to enjoy the fruits of your labor.

What holds you back? What are you afraid of? Believe in yourself, did you know successful individuals are always working on the process of succeeding despite objections? Just think, Thomas Edison tried 1,000 times to invent the light bulb. Most people quit after one or two tries. Give yourself credit and be confident by maximizing every opportunity to succeed because that next step might be the one to finally open the door to your dreams.

Mind of the Million Dollar Ninjas

"Be a master of mind rather than mastered by mind"

- Zen Proverb

When I was a young boy, I was invited to a friend's house for a birthday party. His father was a successful lawyer, and lived in a large house on the wealthy side of our area. I distinctly remember walking through the doors for the first time in awe of the large staircase, multiple rooms, and the huge entertainment area. I thought to myself what a lucky guy, here my family was struggling to meet our daily food needs while my friend was enjoying the lap of luxury. Their world seemed so far away for us, almost unreachable. I kept telling myself someday I hope to have that as well in my life.

As soon as I left the party, I excitedly told my parents of how grand my friend's house was. My parents smiled and said someday you can do it too if you work hard enough for it.

Almost a decade later, I re-connected with the same friend at university. I told him how much I envied his lifestyle when we were kids. It was at this point he informed me that it was all an illusion. In fact, his father was deeply in debt, forcing him to declare bankruptcy. Not only did he lose his business, but his house and marriage at the same time.

This was a wakeup call for me. So many people out there give off this illusion of success. They drive fancy cars, wear designer brands, and play the part of the successful millionaire. However, many are mortgaged up to their ears, and owe thousands if not millions to the bank just to keep up with their image.

In the book, The Millionaire Mind by Thomas J. Stanley, his research revealed that most millionaires in the United States live like regular people. They don't drive the fancy cars instead opting to live in modest homes while saving their money in wise investments. Too many of us get mislead by what is truly success.

A number of years ago, my father had a stopover in Vancouver where he met up with a childhood friend, whom he hadn't seen since they were kids. His friend had grown up poor in Hong Kong, and as an adult he set up a toy factory in China eventually becoming a multi-millionaire. Truly a great rags to riches story. After their reunion, my father noted that even though his friend was successful and worth so much now, he was wearing a plain white Haynes T-shirt with a hole in it. My father laughed, reflecting that his friend hadn't changed much at all.

In my experience, many of the true successful people I've come across in my life are like black belt masters, humble in their approach, rarely displaying their success to others. They understand the rocky journey to get there, the long days of working, rarely seeing their family or taking time off to relax. They scale one mountain only to find another mountain ahead to climb. They develop extremely thick skin to conquer roadblocks on their path to success in order to keep moving forward, never once backing down from challenges.

Most successful business entrepreneurs have never taken martial arts but many have a black belt mentality, using it wisely to propel them to the next level. One important thing that black belts masters have in common with millionaires is they know there is no such thing as an overnight success. Both realize the journey to success can be a long one often filled with many set-backs and disappointments along the way. They will be knocked down over and over again but the ones who succeed will get up, brush themselves off, and continue to move forward with steely determination. The weak-willed, on the other hand, will run away when things become difficult. It's at this moment when that inner voice tells you to run away especially when you encounter greater difficulties. Tell yourself, this is your time to shine, you will not give in to your inner critic, not this time because your dream is just a peering around the corner, waiting for you to grab it by the handles.

This black belt mentality is what the martial arts has stressed for years. It's no wonder martial arts schools are popular for their kids' programs. Parents want their kids to develop confidence, discipline, and a sense of drive. The belt ranking system gives them something tangible to strive for, while the continual mastering of techniques allows them to see their personal growth on a daily basis. As a teacher, there is nothing like seeing a student's face light up when they finally execute a technique they have struggled with.

To develop the black belt mentality, one must be able to manage their thoughts. I want you to start taking ownership of this important concept. Be the CEO or president of your thoughts instead of being the employee who follows the orders. Put yourself in control by becoming a leader instead of a follower.

It is believed we have as many as a thousand thoughts racing through our mind each day. Many of these thoughts are often repetitive in nature. Perhaps it could be a painful childhood experience that keeps replaying itself over and over again. From childhood to adulthood, our brain gathers and stores our personal experiences, both good and bad. This store house of information acts as our personal database. It can serve us in a great way by helping us avoid potential dangerous situations based on past experiences. On the other hand, it can restrain us from fulfilling our potential by replaying emotional experiences for example, public speaking or the fear of rejection can force us into our shell. By staying in this shell we will never know what we are capable of. As a result, we could be losing out on some of the biggest opportunities of our lives. Just imagine if someone like Oprah Winfrey gave up broadcasting after getting fired from a local TV station, where would she be today? We would never have heard of her, and her message would not have reached millions of people.

Be mindful of these thoughts you have flowing through your head each day as our current perception of life is due to these past events whether negative or positive. One of the things I love to do is have a sit down conversation with my inner thoughts, like sitting down with a friend over coffee at a local Starbucks.

Like any conversation, we can have a friendly debate over certain issues. Ask your inner critic is this information you are providing me at this moment really true? Will it harm or hurt me if I don't listen to it? What are the consequences if I don't listen to it? What are the benefits if I ignore it?

I've found that many of the thoughts we have are usually nothing to worry about, and they are irrational thoughts. Usually they are long standing fears that have accumulated from our childhood which hold us back as adults. Our current perception of life can be blamed on these past events both positive and negative.

One of the biggest challenges I had to overcome was constant worry. Often I would lay awake at night thinking of all the things that could potentially go wrong in my life. It caused me incredible anxiety and stress for many years. This habit was passed on to me by my mother who was constantly worried about me when I was growing up. To protect me, she kept me from participating in normal kid activities. She was constantly worrying about this person or that person. Her worries were not based on truth but what was running through her imagination at the time. I often ask her why she worried about these frivolous things because they cannot be controlled. Just enjoy life and the finer moments it brings.

Through years of training, black belts can calmly execute techniques under stressful conditions. They have trained their mind to be calm, blocking out the distractions around them as they laser focus on their opponent. This strategy allows them to shift to another technique when the opponent changes course. You can implement this concept in your daily life but understand that you own your thoughts. You control all your thoughts, no one else can. Your happiness, your dreams, how to you behave, are all under your domain. Don't let other people's negative perceptions and view of the world influence your own thoughts. Controlling these thoughts can have a profound effect on how great your life can be. Create the masterpiece you've always envisioned for yourself. You dictate the pace, leading the way to success.

When I spar in martial arts, I never worry about what my opponent is going to do because he will do what he wants to regardless of what I think. The difference of whether I get the upper hand or not is based on how quickly I can impose my game on them. Build a positive attitude with the same zest as a martial arts fighter, take control of the action quickly, dominating from start to finish. Be relentless, never letting up until you've become the best you can be.

Martial arts masters and millionaires both abide by one important lesson. They never assume that a technique or business idea will fail. They don't dwell on past mistakes, instead opting to think about the great rewards of success.

Chapter 9
Positive Attitude

IN SPORTS, PLAYERS WHO exhibit a poor attitude are often referred to as a "cancer'" in the locker room. Their less than desirable behavior often leads to infighting with teammates and coaches, preventing a team from building a winning culture. It is no surprise that organizations who manage the personalities of the players create a long term winning culture. When you think of winning teams in sports, you think of the New York Yankees, Boston Celtics, New England Patriots, or Detroit Red Wings.

Possessing a positive attitude is a key component in building the champion within you. I've seen many people with great technical skills fail to achieve their full potential due to poor attitude. On the flip side, I've taught students who didn't possess natural ability at the beginning, but were able to overcome limitations due to a positive attitude and willingness to learn.

Life can be extremely unfair. One may experience a bankruptcy, divorce, be born with a handicap, or grow up in a disadvantaged community. None of these factors should ever stop anyone from success. Everyone including the wealthiest people on this earth all started at the same point, with nothing. What separated them from the rest of the population is the positive attitude of not letting anything or anyone dictate their success.

As for yourself, what is holding you back from your dreams? Your potential or purpose in life? Are the little voices in your head telling you that you are incapable of such feats? Was it someone, a parent or authority figure, who told you when you were kid that you were not bright enough, beautiful enough, or fast enough to make it to the big leagues in your field?

Walt Disney was fired for being unimaginative. Jerry Seinfeld was fired from a minor role in a sitcom called Benson. Elvis Presley was told by a concert manger he was better off going back to Memphis to drive a truck.

Stop saying, "I wish I can." Start saying, "I can, and I will."

Slay The Dragons

"Quiet the mind and the soul will speak."

Ma Jaya Sati Bhagavati – Spiritual Teacher

A few years ago I headed out for my daily Sunday practice session with my martial arts team. Sunday is what we referred to as open mat classes. There are no formal techniques being taught, just sparring or what we refer to in Brazilian Jiu-jitsu as rolling.

During rolling sessions you and your partner attempt to submit one another. It's a valuable time to hone your technique, understand where your weaknesses lie and to seek improvements. It can also be a test of your character, patience, ego, and mindset.

As I made my way down the steps towards the change rooms, I was greeted by some of my students. It was a warm day, we had about 35 sweaty people in the gym giving it their all. It looked fun, I soon joined in on the action training with the students.

Two hours had passed and the gym owner announced they would be closing the gym in 15 minutes, everyone who wanted to take a shower must do so now. Almost everyone cleared the area immediately. As I made my way to the end of the mat there was one student remaining, a white belt who I shall refer to as Mark. He barked at me, "Hey! You wanna roll?"

I responded with, "the gym is closing in 15 minutes, we need to hit the showers now."

Mark with his sneer barked back, "but it will be quick!"

I had never formally met Mark, but the locker room banter about this individual was that no one liked to train with him. Apparently he was overly aggressive, hurt people, and conducted himself in a strange manner.

Being one of the teachers in the dojo, I wasn't too pleased with the manner he spoke to me. Traditionally lower belts like Mark are not to ask higher belts like myself to spar. It's up to the higher belt to call them over. However, I was not a big traditionalist so it was no big deal, but what irked me was he had the tone of a bully. To me this was unacceptable, and he needed to be taught a valuable lesson. With that I agreed to a sparring match with him.

Within 15 seconds, I landed a choke on him forcing him to tap out. I quickly got up, bowed, thanked him, and started walking away.

He barked, "that's it?"

Knowing he needed a lesson in setting aside his ego, I thought I would push his emotional buttons a little to see if he got my message.

I responded sarcastically, "yes, you wanted a quick match, I gave you a quick match."

His eyes and face began to turn red, you could literally see the steam blowing out of his ears. He felt humiliated by my words, and wanted to make a spectacle of me.

He demanded a rematch slapping the match in anger, "let's go again!"

We quickly engaged again. This time, he found himself flying through the air where I quickly applied a bicep crush, short of breaking his arm. He screamed in pain while tapping out in the process. Holding his arm, he sheepishly shook my hand, thanking me for sparring with him.

A few weeks later he personally apologized to me, thanking me for teaching him a lesson. I explained to him I did not resent him at all but wanted to help him. I told him his behavior in class was unacceptable, for to be a great martial artist one must learn how to conduct themselves in and out of class, with dignity, honor, and integrity.

As we got deeper in our conversation, he recalled how he was bullied as a child. One incident he never forgot was when a kid had jumped on top of him, raining punches down on him as he unsuccessfully tried to defend himself.

Even though he was now in his thirties, those painful memories served as a constant reminder of his vulnerability. I now understood why he needed to feel like the dominant student in class. He was unable to let go of a past experience which continued to affect his behavior.

As a coach, a lot can be discovered about an individual during these sessions. How they handle defeat, do they get angry, do they injure their training partners, do they take losing personally? I've seen students almost come to blows during open rolling sessions which in my opinion violates one of the core principles in martial arts that is to be respectful.

On the flip side, I've seen students grow from the experience of losing each class. They accept defeat as the opportunity to ask the teachers what is needed to reach the next level in their journey. Often when they join they are timid, shy, or unsure of themselves. After a few months, they are helping beginner students integrate into the system.

For many decades, I've seen all types of students come and go in the martial arts schools. Some have egos that don't allow them to grow, while others accept new challenges as learning opportunities.

I've often observed what makes certain students act the way they do during times of perceived threat and competition. When a student acts up in class, many complain quietly about the individual's behavior behind the scenes.

However, I like to sit down with that student to dig into their past history a little to find out the reasons behind their behavior. More often or not it can be traced back to an incident or a serious of childhood traumatic events that created a core belief they have not learned to let go as an adult.

Do you have dragons from the past that keep holding you back from taking calculated risks, risks that may bring you rewards you never dreamt of? Are the dragons continuing to surround you every day, keeping you away from the gates to the future?

Do you continue to run away from these dragons, sometimes returning to fight but only end up turning back the other way because it's too much of an uphill battle for you to take on?

Slay your dragons one by one every day until you knock the fortress down. It's here you will have jumped a major hurdle in your life, giving you the self-confidence to side step future obstacles.

Demons Be Gone

"Tell the negative committee that meets inside your head to sit down and shut up."

Ann Bradford – Author

What can we learn about mindset from top league athletes? Often times, it is their mental state that determines whether or not they will be successful in life. We've seen in professional sports come playoff time, a team that has performed extremely well in the regular season get eliminated in the first round of the playoffs by a lower seeded team. Some teams or individuals are never able to master their inner game thus they are never able to experience championship success. While others are able to set aside less than ideal life experiences to master winning in life.

Inner chatter, is the downfall for many of us when our greatest performance is needed. When the pressure is on, with all eyes on you, are you able to rise to the occasion? These world class athletes know how to elevate themselves to be the best in their field. Some seem to do it naturally without hesitation or self-doubt while others struggle withering under pressure.

Champions never shy from a challenge. They re-assess what they did wrong the first time, making adjustments to make another run at the prize. They are able to turn challenges into a game of chess, a maze of fun obstacles offering new insights waiting eagerly to be solved. However, most people slam their fist on the table in frustration, preferring to walk away as the challenge becomes too great for them to bare.

Some of you may have had tremendous challenges growing up. Some blame their misfortunate on the lack of luck, on their parents, or on events that happened many years ago. Others credit those experiences for building their inner drive to succeed.

Too often we believe our future is determined by our past. We remember an authority figure telling us we were not good enough, perhaps it may have been an embarrassing moment in school which has left residual hurt and hasn't subsided.

Our brains houses the amygdala, it is here where our experiences are stored. When we experience a stressful moment our experiences are drawn from this place in our brain, causing us to either fight or flight. It's the main reason why many of us revert back to what we are comfortable with when we face adversity. Our past experience tells us we are in danger, protect yourself and run away. While it is good to have this built in alarm system, we need to determine whether we are truly in danger. In ancient times, humans had to defend themselves everyday against animals or rival tribes. However, today in most countries we are not at war but we still have this evolutionary trait preventing us from accepting challenges that will bring us the greatest rewards.

It is not easy to rid yourself of inner chatter. Most of us don't even know how we are limiting ourselves by letting it control our everyday life. I myself only started to realize in my twenties how I kept myself from success. I could no longer blame my parents or the life challenges that occurred while in my childhood.

I'm not the only one who has difficulties in getting rid of inner chatter. Bill Wolfe, one of my self-defense instructors, served in peace keeping missions with the United Nations. He told me how even to this day - 40 years later - his horrific memories of war can be triggered by a certain smell or a Vietnamese or Middle Eastern accent.

Once when I was competing at the Pan Americans tournament in Los Angeles I saw a teammate of mine that I hadn't seen in a while. He was a highly skilled fighter, at least from my experience with him at the dojo. To my surprise he told me he wasn't competing that day. He used to beat all the students in the gym, yet he wasn't competing at one of the most prestigious tournaments of the year.

He explained to me that he doesn't perform well at tournaments. He experienced multiple losses in past tournaments because he was unable to control his emotions during the matches. As I listened, I thought back to the times I trained with him. Indeed, he was definitely talented but he also didn't like to be beaten in class. Occasionally someone would get the upper hand on him causing him to respond with anger. Unfortunately, this student was a prime example of great physical abilities but a lack of mental acuity.

Great martial artists first and foremost know how to keep their emotions in check. Before reacting, they have learned how to clear the mind, allowing them to make the best possible decision. They are also trained to block out distractions around them to ensure a laser focus on their goals.

What is your negative self-talk or inner critic telling you? How are the people around you affecting how you feel about yourself? Are you happy with what you have accomplished in life so far?

If not, what are the excuses holding you back? Are all those reasons really valid? Take time to write down all the reasons and begin creating a new exciting life for yourself. Start eliminating the irrational reasons one by one starting today. Get rid of your inner demons forever.

Chapter 10
Vision

A WHILE BACK, I was looking through old photo albums from my dad's younger days as a martial artist. One photo that stood out was his teacher great grandmaster Fong meditating at the temple in Hong Kong. The practice of visualization and meditation has been used for centuries as a way of clearing the mind to focus on goal achievement. In fact, the use of visualization is deeply rooted in Chinese culture. My parents always had a glass sculpture of three Chinese children pulling a cart of gold. This was carefully placed near the front entrance of our house to symbolize bringing wealth and good fortune to our household.

I used to scoff at the idea. How could this possibly work? After all, we struggled for many years just to pay the bills. I ended up eating my words as years later the family business went from a struggling mom and pop home business to a major player in the Chinese produce industry in Manitoba.

Master Fong practicing meditation in Hong Kong circa 1960

The question for some of the skeptics is does visualization really work? There have been studies to prove its effectiveness. One interesting study was done with a basketball team. They had one group practice free throw shooting and visualization while the other group just shot free throws. The one that incorporated visualization into their practice outshot the group who didn't use it.

High level athletes from Olympic athletes, musicians, successful business people all incorporate visualization as a part of their success routine. Visualization is a powerful tool to implement it into your daily routine.

See It to Believe It

Never assume because a man that has no eyes he cannot see. Close your eyes. What do you hear?

– Master Po, Kung Fu the TV series

In 2010, I had just been awarded my purple belt in Brazilian Jiu-jitsu by my instructor Todd Nathanson in Los Angeles. One day, I came in for my regularly scheduled private lesson with him and his son Jared.

As we got ready to get physical and down to business, they sat me down on the mats. The tone in their voice softened to almost a whisper, quiet as if they wanted to share a secret with me. They asked me if I did any reading and visualization. I looked at them strangely and said no. They responded by saying that not many people do visualization exercises but it will be one of the most important things you need to do now that you are approaching the black belt level.

I was then asked, what do you see when you're sparring? I replied that I see a series of highways with detours everywhere. Interesting, they added they saw a grassy field meadow with a steady wind blowing gently across it.

Todd and Jared spent the next 60 minutes talking to me about this concept without showing me one physical technique. When the lesson was over they asked if I understood, I sheepishly said yes, but a part of me inside of myself asked what the heck was that? I can't believe I just spent $150 for a private lesson where we just talked! I felt ripped off as I drove away from the academy.

When I got back to my hotel room to retire for the evening I began to think about what they had taught me. Keeping an open mind, I began incorporating daily visualization into my jiu-jitsu training. A few months later I noticed a significant improvement in my game. Suddenly, all my senses became more heightened, things that used to be fast slowed down for me. It was almost like I was in a constant dream state during sparring, a Zen like state. It was an exciting moment, and it turned out to be the most important private lesson I learned from my teacher.

Sharing a light hearted moment with my teacher Master Todd Nathanson

As I researched the power of visualization, I noticed every successful person used it as a tool to help them achieve their goals. Sports teams, entrepreneurs, millionaires, billionaires, musicians, and Olympians. They practice their routines in their head, rehearsing each step over and over again.

There have been documented accounts of prisoners of war learning how to play musical instruments while in captivity for many years despite not having physical instruments to play with.

The brain is an incredible organ when used to its highest potential. Unfortunately, most of us do not take the time to maximize its capabilities and what it can do for us if we feed it with the right information.

Before he became famous, actor comedian Jim Carrey wrote a check to himself for 10 million dollars, and placed it in his wallet as a daily reminder of his goal. As you all know, Jim went on to become one of Hollywood's highest paid actors.

One of the visualization tools I enjoy doing is a vision board. Take a piece of cardboard, print or cut out photos from the magazine of all the things you want in your life. Glue them on this board, pin the board somewhere you can see it every day. I like to use my office as I spend the majority of my time there. Not only does it serve as a constant reminder of why I do what I do but it also keeps me on a straight path towards my goals. Like a GPS, it repositions me back on the road when I begin to veer off my mission. Some people place the vision board on the ceiling above their bed so they can fall asleep with a vision of their dreams.

In addition, you can hang any awards you have accomplished on the same wall. This allows you to celebrate your success when you are feeling down or face a challenge on your road to achieving excellence.

You not only have to see the images, but tune in to your other senses. What do you smell when you get that new car? The leather and the freshness of a new car. What does it feel like when you drive it? What does it sound like? What is the color?

Quit watching negative news, violent movies, or listening to angry music before bed. Instead, start filling your head with positive images. When you see what you want, your brain will do all the necessary things to pool its resources together for you to get it. I find with regular practice so many new ideas are generated every day. Don't let your talents go to waste. Make this life your greatest.

Chapter 11
Leadership

THERE IS THE OLD myth that great leaders are born not made. The problem is many of us don't believe we can be great leaders. We look around us at the people we admire, believe they have this superhuman skill they were lucky to be born with while the rest of us got the leftovers.

The great news is leadership is a skill you can learn through study, practice and effort. Successful people know how to lead, and they never rest on past successes nor do they dwell on past failures.

One trait of all great leaders is their natural curiosity to learn and study everything in their field to achieve mastery. A great basketball player studies the greats before them. Michael Jordan studied Dr. J, Kobe Bryant studied Michael Jordan.

What can you do in your career to be the best performer in your department or company? As a student, what skills would you need to propel you to the top of the class? What about the other areas in your life?

Before I received my black belt I asked myself these very questions every day. What are my weaknesses, what are successful competitors doing that I am not currently doing, how can I acquire those skills, and which mentors can help me get to the next level more quickly?

Ask yourself these very same questions, write them down as a reminder, and do everything in your power to recruit the necessary resources to get you to your goal.

Spend Each Day Training to Be the Best

"Every day I strive to, at least, recognize my short-comings and the things I have to do to be the best person that I can possibly be."

Alexander O'Neal – American Blues Singer

In 2006, I made the decision to learn from the top Brazilian Jiu-Jitsu fighters in the world. One of them was a legend living in Los Angeles named Jean Jacques Machado. Upon arriving at his academy I couldn't help but be in awe of the accolades lining the front office and throughout the school, trophies, medals, and magazines of him gracing the front cover.

As I made myself on to the mats, I saw Ricco Rodriquez who was the reigning UFC heavyweight champion at the time, and Joe Rogan, the host of Fear Factor and UFC commentator. The quality of the students was something I had never experienced before; there was an elite championship quality to it. The skill level, and the school's culture to foster the cultivation of excellence was definitely noticeable.

This experience shifted my thinking on what it took to become the best I could be. The greatness in that studio was not only reserved for the elite champions in the gym, but I found the regular students to be extremely sound and technical in Jiu-Jitsu.

I was so impressed I began travelling down there two to three times per year to train. It was there that I met my teacher and jiu-jitsu mentor Professor Todd Nathanson. I observed the way he taught, how his students responded, and asked every question that came to mind on how to succeed in the art. Slowly I became immersed in learning everything I could to become a high level practitioner. Practices included three to four hour practices, followed by the study of videos for another five hours - often keeping me up to 3 am. Off days were followed by weight lifting, massage sessions and stretching.

Jiu-jitsu became my full-time passion, and I loved every minute of it. Over the years as a result of the training, my attitude towards achieving human potential began to shift to other areas in my life. The martial arts lessons of perseverance, discipline, and the focus on constant daily improvement became a way of living.

I was never an avid reader growing up but suddenly found myself reading books on leadership, self-improvement, and business. The interesting thing was the more self-educated I became the more money I made; I became a better competitor, and handled challenges completely differently.

Look deep inside of yourself to ask if you truly did everything possible today to become better. If not, what is lacking? More education? Do you need to change the team or people who are around you most of the day? These people might not have the skills required to push you to the next level. There is a saying, "if you want to be a millionaire, hang out with a millionaire." If you want to become an Olympic athlete, you train with the best program on the planet.

Treat your life and future like a high school track star looking to compete in the Olympic games one day. What are they doing each day to make that dream become a reality? They put 100% into practice on and off the field every day. Use this model for your daily life to help your reach milestones you never thought possible.

Chapter 12
Humility

ONE OF THE KEY lessons I share with my students, especially the beginners, is to always be humble. No one knows everything, although some act like they do. I have yet to find someone who does, and if you know someone please let me know because I would like to meet that individual one day.

One characteristic of being humble is to always ask questions. Seems simple but for many it's hard to do. Sometimes questions are uncomfortable – think of a student needing the help of a teacher or an employee asking a boss for a day off. Perhaps it was a horrible childhood experience that makes us fear being judged, laughed at, or worse, hearing the word no.

Nobody enjoys this feeling, and after experiencing it a number of times we prefer to not ask questions at all for fear of feeling hurt. Whether you are asking someone out on a date, making a sales call, or asking for a favor, to get anything in life you need to ask the question. By not asking you have in fact rejected yourself before knowing what the answer may be. To move the needle of success forward or to even set it in motion we must learn to ask without fear. Not everything will be a yes but if you ask enough, chances are you will get a yes.

Take for instance these famous people who asked and were rejected multiple times before finding success:

- Charles Schultz, the famous cartoonist for Peanuts, had every cartoon he submitted rejected by his high school year book.

- Kentucky Fried Chicken founder Colonel Sanders was rejected by 1,009 restaurants before finding an interested party for his now world famous chicken recipe.

In fact, studies show 20% of the top salespeople make 80% of the money. Why is this? It's because close to half of the salespeople give up after the first call. They say it takes roughly 5 calls before a sale is made.

Back when I was a kid, a gentleman from Denver wanted to sell my father an alfalfa sprout machine. It took 2 years of him calling along with countless thank you, not right now replies from my father before he got a yes. My father was impressed by this man's persistence. Thirty-four years later my father has bought over a million dollars' worth of equipment from him, forging a lifelong business relationship.

As I always tell my students every class; "the question you think is stupid or the one you don't ask, is usually the one everyone wants answered."

Never Assume, Just Ask

"Asking for help with shame says: You have the power over me. Asking with condescension says: I have the power over you. But asking for help with gratitude says: We have the power to help each other."

Amanda Palmer – Author

When I was child, I was often screamed at by my mother for asking for things. She didn't handle stress very well and often her temper would boil over towards me. Simply asking to stay over an extra night at my cousin's place would result in a stern loud reprimand. This happened so often throughout my childhood that over time the once cheerful trustful expressive kid that I was began to turn inward, becoming awkwardly shy and quiet. At the time, I couldn't understand why a simple request warranted such a harsh response. I associated this response with bad behavior, that I was somehow wrong for asking in the first place. By the time I reached my teens, I had stopped asking my parents for anything, even when things were troubling me. At times, I felt helpless, unable to turn to anyone for my problems so I kept them inside. For years, this holding back of emotions turned into anger, bitterness, and manifested in problematic health conditions such as anxiety, eczema, and stress.

The message I picked up from my mom was don't ask for anything because you are a nuisance. This message became loud and clear. At a young age, I stopped asking for help from teachers in school feeling I would be wasting their time for not understanding the assignment. Often I sat through classes staring at a blank sheet of paper while the rest of the kids were writing away. I was too ashamed to ask for help for fear of being scolded like I was at home. It was an experience that was painful back then, bringing up a host of emotions when I think about it today. I witness many kids have their spirits broken at a young age sometimes by their parents or a poor teacher at school.

By the time they grow up they become timid, unsure of themselves, lacking the right skills to maximize their potential in helping them excel in the world. A big part of the success process is leveraging the power of asking. When you are taught at a young age that asking is a bad thing, you are teaching your child to follow, not lead. They now relegate the success (or lack thereof) in their life to the hands of fate. In simple terms, you need to ask to receive or get what you want in life. Keep in mind all because you ask doesn't mean it will always result in a yes. There will be rejections along the way but that is the beauty of it. At least you know and you never leave any stone unturned or lose out on any potential opportunities.

Take for instance, buying a new car. How many times do you see one person leave the car lot who pays more but receives less add-on features compared to a savvier negotiator who pays the lowest price but gets some added features thrown in for free? It is because they ask! Too few of us do so because we fear being rejected, we feel embarrassed to ask as we are conditioned to not like the word no. Thus we end off short changing ourselves.

One time, one of my young students asked me about dating. He said he had trouble asking girls out because he was rejected one time in front of the other high school kids. Since then he has crawled into a shell.

My response to him was, if I got you to stand on the street corner for a few hours, smile and ask every girl that walked by if they would like to join you for coffee, how many would say yes?

He said, maybe none but most likely at least one.

I said, okay but if you didn't stand on the corner to ask preferring to stay safe from rejection, how many would join you for a cup of java?

Well none, he said.

My lesson to him was to take a chance there is no harm. You have nothing so even if you didn't get one date you lost nothing in the first place.

Look at how you can apply this concept to your everyday life as an adult. For example, cold calling to build your sales, asking for a raise, negotiating a better interest rate for your credit card, or asking for a better seat in a restaurant.

When I became an adult, I was paralyzed by fear to ask. I did things by myself even when I needed help such as moving to another home. Finally, when successful mentors came into my life, I got a reality check as I discovered that their biggest reason for success was their unwavering ability to ask anyone for anything.

One of the things that have been really huge for me was thinking bigger when it came to asking for things such as celebrity endorsements or asking CEOs for advice. Some have given me an answer and some have not but the main point is that I reached out and connected with some important people – connections that I wouldn't have dreamed of having if I let fear hold me back.

Too often we put celebrities or people in positions of power on a pedestal, fearing that we are not worthy of their time. I'm going to tell you today you are more than worthy; in fact, you owe it to yourself if you truly want to be the best.

Keep in mind that these powerful people started just like you and I. Most came from extremely humble beginnings. Oprah Winfrey came from extreme poverty, was fired from a TV station, and today is one of the wealthiest women in the world.

Bruce Lee was rejected by every Hollywood movie studio. He was told an Asian movie actor was not bankable. They couldn't have been more wrong as he went on to become the greatest martial arts legend to ever lived.

So stop hiding in the corner, get in on the action, and start getting out of life what you deserve. Start asking at every opportunity you get. Remember, when you do get that ever so important request filled, do yourself a favor and send a thank you card to that person to show gratitude.

Chapter 13
Courage

A BIG PART OF being a success in my opinion is the ability to stand up for yourself and make a positive impact in society or your community. There can be a fear associated with taking this on - a fear of failure, confrontation, or rejection.

We often underestimate ourselves as small individuals who don't possess the star or celebrity power to make a difference in this world. Our little voice in our head tells us "who am I?"

I wasn't Mr. Popular in school. In fact, I would describe myself as very mediocre and painfully shy. Let's say those years were not the most memorable.

One painful experience came in grade 8, when a friend and I made the final rounds at the annual regional Science Fair. Our teacher at the time dropped by to speak to us before the evaluators came around. At first I thought he wanted to give us some words of encouragement. To my dismay, he told me to leave when the evaluators came to judge our project, adding he didn't want to ruin the chances of my friend winning the competition.

Hurt and fuming inside, I composed myself holding back the tears as my friend watched in shock. I never forgot that day, and I can still see this teacher's heartless expression even now, more than 30 years later. It's what drives me every day to get up in the morning to help others who are dismissed.

What drives you? What challenges did you struggle with growing up or recently where you can make a difference? Maybe it wasn't you with a challenge - it could be a relative or friend who was diagnosed with a life threatening disease. It could also be animals, the environment, or politics.

Get involved and leave this earth a better place then we you came into it.

You Don't Need to Be a Famous to Make an Impact

"You may think your light is small, but it can make a big difference in other people's lives. Let your light shine."

- Unknown

When I was young, I would pretend to be like my idol master arts master Bruce Lee, and think about what it would be like to be someone famous on TV. I guess I was no different than any other imaginative kid dreaming about life in the big spot light. We have all dreamed about this one time in our life; however, most of us never believe getting to that level is possible for us so we never bother to try.

While being a celebrity truly helps gets your message across the masses a lot more quickly, rest assured you don't have to be famous to make your impact felt with others. There are countless people everyday who do great things, impacting the lives of others without getting noticed by the press. This would include doctors, police officers, nurses, teachers, and even martial artists like myself.

Helping empower female youth groups through martial arts.

One of the most touching moments of my career is hearing from past clients who email me out of the blue sometimes 10 years after I have coached them, to tell me how much I have changed their life for the better. I can't begin to tell you how that makes me feel. I have to pinch myself, asking why me? How can this be? I was a once a young kid who was dismissed by others as having little value, and to now be credited with changing the lives of many it seems so surreal.

I remember fumbling my words when I spoke to someone more senior than me in business, or feeling extremely nervous when attending a black tie event in the company of famous authors, producers, or elite athletes, believing I wasn't deserving.

When I was 16 years old in 1985, I attended a track meet in Saskatchewan. It was the first time I had travelled away from home and got to room with some of my teammates. The track meet also featured some of Canada's best sprinters at the time, one being Ben Johnson who was later disqualified from the 1988 Olympics for using banned steroids.

Before this unfortunate incident, Ben was a hero to Canadians especially to a young runner like myself. I will never forget that weekend when I got to see him run in the 60-meter event. As the sprinters blasted out of the blocks, Ben steamrolled to victory. These world class sprinters were running so fast they leaned a crash mat against the wall near the finish line because many of the sprinters were not able to stop in time. The crash mat helped break their momentum upon crossing the finish line. It was exciting and a real treat to watch them in action.

That night back at our hotel room, we heard a knock on our door and one of my teammates answered it. I asked who it was when he quickly ran back and with excitement softly muttered, oh my gosh, it's Ben Johnson!

The four of us quickly ran to the door, giggling like a bunch of girls as we poked our heads out the door. Ben was surprised at our reaction but amused at the same time and cracked a little smile. With his thick Jamaican accent, he said, "do you know where I can find your coaches?"

"Oh yes, yes Ben, they are in the room beside us," we shouted.

When was the last time you saw a celebrity? How did you react? With nervousness? Are you normally a confident person only to be reduced to a pile of mush upon conversing with them?

How about just a local celebrity such as a news anchor, or someone who is wildly successful? Do you feel you are not worthy of their time?

It's easy to put people of status on a pedestal while reducing our own self-worth. We tend to believe they are superhuman, doing things no one else is able to do. And we turn around to discount all the things that make us special and great.

If everyone in the world would share their gifts with others, this world would be a much better place. Remember, everyone who has reached the top started with nothing. Where would the civil rights movement be if Martin Luther King Jr. decided he was too small to make an impact?

Never believe you are too small to make a difference in this world. Step out today to make a difference in the lives of others around you, in your community, and the world. You may not change the entire world but you can certainly touch people in your community. Volunteer for causes you believe in, change the lives of a child or a family and make a difference instead of maintaining the status quo.

Not only will you feel great doing it but you are helping others succeed in life as well. In turn, share this commitment to giving by inspiring the ones you help to do the same for others.

Chapter 14
Honor

THE CONCEPT OF HONOR IS highly emphasized in martial arts training. It is here that the master carefully assesses the character of a student, deciding whether a student displays the outstanding character to carry on the traditions of the art. This analysis goes beyond physical strengths, taking into consideration the attitude they display in and out of the dojo.

Do they help out their fellow classmates, display a positive attitude, and are they mentally strong enough to stay out of trouble with the law?

When my father was teaching in the 1970s, he adhered to this time tested tradition. Many of his top students went on to become extremely successful after their rambunctious teenage years. I recall one student who built a software company and eventually sold it for millions. Another troubled teen became a well-known highly successful oral surgeon.

This principle of honor has never been lost on me. I spent many hours observing my students away from the action. I also talk to them long enough to know what they do outside of the gym and what kind of people they socialize with. It is who they socialize with largely determines how they behave in and out of the class. It's actually quite interesting watching and listening to all of them.

The elite students who do well in business, career, and are very happy and do not waste time hanging around negative toxic people. They come in, do their work out and then leave when it is time. Their inner circle of friends are equally successful or on their way to success.

These students know what they want in life, where they are going to, and they exhibit a strong sense of awareness on how the people around them affect their attitude.

On the flip side, there are the students who live a life of constant turmoil. They constantly complain, often seem unsettled, blame others or offer excuses, and take joy in gossiping. Their minds seem to always be somewhere else rather than enjoying the moment.

Nobody likes a complainer or whiner. Successful people know what they want and execute their plan to the best of their ability.

Step back for a minute, and think about all the people in your life. Are they adding value to your life? Are they lifting you up or are they bringing you down? The group you socialize or hang out with can impact your success.

Think back to your high school days - everyone remembers that one popular guy or girl everyone wanted to be friends with. We followed their lead because it was the popular thing to do. Fast forward many years later and you may discover that the most popular person in your high school became a nobody in life. We wonder why we wasted our time looking up to this individual. They may have been a fun person to be around in terms of partying but how did following this person make you a better person?

Spend time with people who contribute positive vibes to your life. Do they add value? Do you have meaningful conversations? Do they have great suggestions for you? Do they encourage you wholeheartedly? Are they willing to extend their hand out to help you succeed rather than withhold information for fear they would be left behind if you succeed?

These are powerful questions you need to determine for yourself on the company you decide to keep in your life.

Stop Feeling You're Entitled to A Great Life

"The time to strike is when the opportunity presents itself"

– Tatsuo Shimabuku

Jimmy Butler is one of the best basketball players in the NBA today, known for his smooth shooting stroke, and his tenacious defense, the Chicago Bulls star couldn't be in a better place in his career. You would think that

Jimmy the all-star was blessed with God given talent and had an easy road to NBA success.

However, this couldn't have been farther from the truth. Many years ago, the NBA was only a distant dream for him. Just surviving day to day was the ultimate challenge.

He grew up fatherless from an early age and he was kicked out of his home by the age of 13 by his mother who claimed she didn't like the way he looked. With no money to live on, he made his way through a serious of foster homes.

When he was a senior in high school, he was taken in by the Leslie family. This provided him with some structure allowing him to focus on school and basketball after years of instability.

While attending high school, his coach didn't believe Jimmy had the basketball skills to succeed in college. As a result, he was not heavily recruited by Division 1 colleges (the top tier). Instead of listening to his coach's opinion, he enrolled in a nearby junior college to hone his basketball skills. Quickly, the big schools took notice of his great skills which eventually led to a scholarship at Marquette University.

In 2011, the Chicago Bulls selected him in the 1st round of the NBA draft, 30th overall. Pretty outstanding for a guy who was cast away by his mother as a child and dismissed by his coach for not being good enough.

His story is a shining example of persevering despite the odds. He could have given in to a life of crime or drugs, ending up as another promising young teen falling prey to the streets.

The obstacles he faced along the way to the NBA could have given him every excuse to go off path but he didn't - he stayed true to his dream for success. He was a model of persistence in pursuit of excellence, never letting his past determine his future outcome.

He could have blamed his mom for his challenges, choosing to dwell on the negative, making excuses about why he was not more successful in high school. Instead, he chose to focus on the one thing he could control and that was his mindset, his play on the court, and his personal development.

World class performers, high achievers, award winning musicians, and CEOs do not spend time complaining about why they deserve something more than others. They never complain that things are not fair or that life has done them wrong. Many people believe they are owed a great life and want to have success handed to them on a silver platter.

Understand that your problems are not unique. There are others out there who have the exact problems as you, some even worse. Yet, many go through life believing they are the only ones who suffer. Having a victim mentality keeps you from seeing what good lies ahead of you. It keeps you stuck in a movie that continues on auto play.

You may become resentful of your best friend from high school upon hearing he became a self-made millionaire at the age of 26.

Maybe you are jealous of your friend's happy marriage because you and your partner fight constantly.

What about the co-worker who gets the job promotion over you? Do you feel anger towards him/her, do you believe you are more deserving then him or her?

Resorting to a victim mentality doesn't help you get farther ahead. Focus on learning how to deal with setbacks. Look at ways to improve yourself daily and focus on a unique skill set that only you can bring to the table. Sometimes you may not get an opportunity you feel you deserve, but perhaps it may not be your time yet. It could a signal that it's time to find someone who does appreciate your unique talents.

Make Lifestyle Changes

"Surround yourself with people that reflect who you want to be and how you want to feel, energies are contagious."

- Unknown Author

When you look closely look at pro sports champions, you may notice a pattern of the same teams consistently winning year after year. This is no coincidence. Some teams may have more money to invest in high performers, but the ones with the highest payroll don't necessarily win all the time. The team that builds a winning culture is the one that finds themselves most often at the championships. Coaches who lift every player on the team and uses each one's strengths have a greater chance in building a strong team. The collective team efforts have a greater chance of success than just a few top performers. Building this successful foundation comes all the way from the top, from the owner all the way down to the field crew resulting in a winning culture. Examples of such team are the NFL New England Patriots, baseball's New York Yankees, or basketball's San Antonio spurs.

Building a winning culture attracts free agent players who want to play for an organization. No one wants to spend their time on a losing team. Most interesting is what happens when an executive or player is brought in to turn around a losing team. No matter how much success this individual has achieved in his past, it's always a major undertaking. In losing environments, everyone has grown to accept losing, to the point where their subconscious expectations each season almost pre-determines the results. Bringing in successful people can change these long standing attitudes, transforming a low performance franchise and turning it into a winner to be reckoned with.

We see the same thing in business and life. People want to work for successful organizations that are respectful and fair. Corporate cultures that encourage a positive, can-do attitude engages employees. This in turn results in to higher productivity for the company. A more toxic company culture will reflect higher absenteeism rates, employee dissatisfaction, high turnover, and underperforming sales.

When it comes to your life outside of work, what influences are having a negative impact on your success? Have you ever taken an inventory on who you spend your free time with?

There are certain individuals in your life who carry a dark cloud around them all the time. They complain about the weather on a nice sunny day, blame others for their lack of personal responsibility, or engage in endless gossip. How are these people contributing to your success?

Negative words and images bombard us each day through the news, social media feeds, and negative people. Spending time on these activities takes up our mental space, taking away our mental clarity to focus on the most important tasks in our life. I remember the days when I spent an hour or two on Facebook going through news feeds or reading the feeds of others. Many of these feeds I spent time reading were from Facebook friends who weren't even close to me in real life. Yet there I was, consumed with their life. I finally said to myself, this is stupid, why am I reading this feed and why should I care about their life so much. It was clear I was heading in the wrong direction, and it was definitely steering me away from executing the goals that were necessary to create the life I wanted.

I made a choice to clean my Facebook account and use the social platform only for business purposes. I've never looked back as I increased my productivity and spent time on things that were meaningful and beneficial towards me. It also saved me from having to be drawn into the social conversations of people who were more acquaintances than close friends.

I have also made more new face to face connections at networking events surrounding myself with other successful people. In the past, I had a mixed bag of results with meeting individuals at networking events. Some people were uplifting to be around while others sucked the energy out of you with their negativity.

I remember years ago, I was training at a gym that had internal politics all the time. Every two years, there was an argument between the owner and one of the instructors resulting in a revolving door of staff. As a member of the gym I found it hard to find stability and continuity with the changing instructors. Although I enjoyed the friends I had made there I decided to change my training environment. I made the trek down to Los Angeles to a famous academy where I met my future teacher, Todd Nathanson. He ran a drama-free, fostering an environment of stability, humbleness, and a deep respect for others.

The move not only improved my skills but taught me lessons on how to conduct my behavior outside of the gym as well. In fact, the environment had such a positive effect on me that I credit it to changing my life forever. These positive role models allowed me to meet other successful people.

This perspective in positivity influenced me long after my training in LA began. Embracing a more positive life, I noticed, brought me more success. Through more networking, I was introduced to directors, celebrity trainers, and business owners who in turn became my clients. The one trait we all had in common was staying positive. Through these lessons I learned to always surround myself with the most successful people.

If you want to be successful, you need to get rid of the negative influences surrounding you. It can be difficult in the face of adversity to practice self-discipline. It is not easy for those who are impoverished to escape the lure of drugs and easy money through a life of crime. It is the ones who stay away from these influences and find new ones who end up writing their ticket out.

Take an inventory of your environment. Decide who has to go, and which types of people you need to bring in to your life to further your success.

Creating Positive Life Change

Negative people need oxygen like drama...Stay positive, it will take their breath away

- Tony Gaskins Jr., Motivational Speaker

One Saturday afternoon, I sat down on my easy chair in my living room reflecting on my 47 years on this earth. It was a beautiful spring day with the sun beaming through my living room window. I thought about all those years I had practiced martial arts; from the day my father took me to the dojo at age 5 to the class I taught the other day.

As a young child, my father never enjoyed teaching large classes. For most my life I remember him only teaching a select few students, no more than six to a class. Looking back, I realized that the small group allowed him to pass on techniques to the most noble students, the ones who exhibited the greatest moral character. Martial arts schools can often be tainted with unpleasant infighting and politics often over payment for classes, control of the martial arts program, and egos between top students, thus creating a less than positive environment. Certain cliques form dividing the students to the point where often troubled students are asked to leave.

I cannot blame my father for electing to train a small group of students. The smaller group meant fewer students who displayed a negative attitude. These students would not accept responsibility for their actions, blaming others for their troubles. They dwelled on the past whether it was it was being passed over for a promotion, rejected, or growing up in less than ideal circumstances, rather than taking the opportunity to evaluate and improve. Instead of absorbing the lessons of personal development through martial arts to transform themselves into a better human being, they continued along the same mediocre path.

My best students are always the ones who accept defeat as a positive. They strive for excellence inside and outside the dojo. They also have a positive outlook no matter what the circumstances are.

One student who really impressed me was a young kid by the name of Ron Dio. From the first day he stepped into the martial arts school, I knew he was going to be a great student. Not only was he respectful and humble but he had great empathy and concern for others. What I didn't know was his mother was sick with cancer, at the same time he was working a full-time job and making a two-hour commute to train every day. Unfortunately, his mother lost her battle with cancer a year ago. Despite all this, Ron never complained and never felt he was cheated in life. He opted to look at the positives in his life, especially the moments he spent with his mother. He is now a caregiver for his father and is always thinking about how he can make life easier for him.

A martial arts master once told me, "Brazilian jiu-jitsu brings two types of people, the classy and the gutters of society. Aspire to be the classy." Ron clearly is a shining example of this.

He never got involved with the "poor me" group at the gym opting to seek advice from successful people. The poor me group consisted of people who sulked about how bad their life is, complaining to whoever was willing to listen.

Have a look around your environment, are you part of the "poor me" group? Who are your friends? Are they going somewhere in life? Is the environment helping you or holding you back from achieving human excellence?

If you are a part of this "poor me" group, it's time to think about shedding some of this dead weight. Think of yourself like a top CEO of a company, you need to surround yourself with the best executive team possible to maximize your potential. I can bet Bill Gates team doesn't have a group of Debbie Downers who preach negativity at every meeting. Nobody who aspires to getting ahead in life wants to constantly listen to a whiner.

Tune in on the language you and the people around you use. Is it positive or negative? I never let my students use the words, "I can't". It's always "I will" or "I can", and if they are not comfortable with that then I get them to say, "I am in the process of becoming".

This triggers their subconscious mind into improving their own mastery, inching towards their success instead of coming to a dead stop. When you do this you build your momentum. At first it may be slow and painful but as time rolls along, things become easier and move much more quickly. Before you realize it you are standing on top of the mountain, relishing your accomplishments and eager to conquer your next milestone.

Scaling that first mountain is always the most difficult. Surround yourself with highly positive people who will help you reach your highest potential. You may need to spend less time with some of your friends, those that have weighed you down. The same is true in dealing with negative family members. Implement these strategies and you will be well on your way to winning the championship of life.

Chapter 15
Listen

ELITE PERFORMERS KNOW THE value of developing their listening skills. It allows them to understand how a person's words can be of benefit to them. One of the great benefits of becoming a great listener is the ability to make use of feedback from others. Too often or not, we view feedback as a criticism. While sometimes it can be hard to accept and hear, it is ultimately up to us to decide how to use feedback to our advantage.

I was reading an article a few years ago about a conversation between Toronto Raptors General Manager Masai Ujiri and his point guard Kyle Lowry. Kyle was a former #1 draft pick. Despite high hopes for his career, he was traded multiple times, fought with coaches and failed to live up to his potential as a high draft pick.

When he arrived in Toronto, Masai called Kyle into his office for a meeting. It was at this meeting where Masai offered valuable advice to the underperforming Lowry, challenging him to take responsibility for his success.

After that meeting, Kyle transformed his game to the highest level in basketball. For his efforts, he was awarded a new lucrative contract for $12 million per season and selected twice to the NBA all-star.

Whatever was said in that meeting finally got through to the young Lowry. Whereas in the past he knocked heads with coaches unwilling to heed to their advice, somehow Masai was able to strike a chord with him. Let's also give Kyle credit for finally showing the maturity to accept feedback as a positive not a negative. His willingness to listen to others proved to be the turning point in his career, transforming him from a borderline starter to one of the elite players in the NBA.

How do you respond to feedback in your daily life? Do you cringe when someone points out a weakness to you? Do you run away from it, opting to stay stuck in your current situation?

What about getting angry with the person who gave you feedback? Perhaps that information will bring you greater success?

As a coach, one of the most frustrating scenarios is when a student ignores feedback, yet keeps making the same mistakes over and over again. From experience, I've seen lower rank martial arts students dismiss the advice from the higher-ranking black belt students. It is ridiculous to believe a student who has practiced one, two or even five years thinks he/she can ignore the cumulative experience of a black belt who has trained 10 years or a lifetime. Although there are new techniques in Brazilian Jiu-jitsu that come out every year, I can honestly say I always take away new insights from the teachers who've come before me. In moments like these, I have often wondered what it would be like to converse with masters from another era.

The words I love to ask myself are "how can I improve...as a spouse, athlete, business person, coach?" By asking myself this question, my subconscious mind is trained to put me on a never ending cycle of self-reflection, self-improvement and motivation.

Practice more listening and less talking. Hone in on your conversations with others, looking for nuggets of information that can help you become better in life and in your career.

Stop letting your emotions and ego get in the way of your progress. Listening to feedback is one of the greatest assets to self-mastery and elite performance enhancement. The sooner your embrace it, the faster you will race to the top of the peak.

Open Your Ears

"Most people do not listen with the intent to understand; they listen with the intent to reply."

– Stephen Covey, American Educator

In the summer of 2011, I flew to Los Angeles for some martial arts training with my teacher Todd Nathanson. I had just completed a two successful years of competing by placing and winning major tournaments. There was talk amongst fellow students that I was going to be promoted to my next belt which was brown belt. The brown belt is a significant achievement as the next level after that is the prestigious black belt. I knew this was not going to be an easy feat as my teacher has very high standards, only promoting students after years of training.

During the week, he spent time putting me in different scenarios during sparring to see how I reacted. For the most part I did fairly well but deep inside I could see there were still major holes in my game. In other schools, I may have gotten a pass to the next level but Master Todd believed in maintaining and upholding the integrity of the belting process. There would be no free passes, no bribery, only hard work that would move him.

On my last day before flying home to Vancouver, he sat me down for a heart to heart conversation. "I'm going to be honest with you," he said. "I know you have been performing well in tournaments and you do some really great things but this one part of your game is completely hideous. I know this must hurt to hear this but I cannot promote you at this time. Go back to Canada and come back next year. I want you to always be prepared for the next level. I don't want you to be the brown belt or black belt who sits in the corner, avoiding the difficult fighters, and only seeking out people you know you can beat."

As I sat there listening, I managed to crack a smile. I told him, "Todd, I'm not hurt. Thank you for your feedback and your honesty. I want to be great and confident at what I do. I promise to get to work immediately on my weaknesses as soon as I arrive back home."

For the remainder of the year, I spent time training with some of the best martial arts performers in my city, working on my weaknesses day after day. It wasn't long before I started manhandling the brown belts, and some of the black belts. Not bad for a 42-year-old I told myself. Before I knew it, some of the senior students started commenting on my advanced prowess, and indicating that I should really be moving up from my purple belt to brown belt. At this time, I knew deep down that I was ready for the next step. About a year later, with the blessing of Master Todd, I was awarded my brown belt.

It was all possible because of how I responded to his feedback positively to achieve my goal. Master Todd kept me on course, and today I am truly better for it.

I use this lesson of listening for feedback to drive my personal excellence in everyday life, applying it wherever I see possible. When I was looking to practice my public speaking skills, I joined a local Toastmasters group known for its laid back and friend atmosphere. Looking to stretch my boundaries more, I asked one of the members if there were other Toastmaster groups I could join. I felt it was important to challenge myself by facing a new unfamiliar group each week. The member gave me a puzzled look and replied that there were many chapters to join but that some of them were harsher with their evaluations than others.

I responded by saying this was exactly what I was looking for. Because I was interested in speaking professionally, not everyone will love me. Some audience members may heckle me; some will be critical. I wanted to learn how to deal with adversity or criticism whether it was warranted or not."

Never look at feedback as a negative thing; rather, look at it as noticing a weakness that you may have overlooked. At times it is hard remain subjective. However, not all feedback is valuable. Think of the friend who gives you financial advice but is always broke, or the acquaintance who gives you relationship advice even though they have a terrible history of being a committed partner.

Make sure the source of feedback comes from an individual who has a proven track record of success. One of the things that annoys me the most when teaching martial arts is hearing a student who never practices, with poor skills, giving advice to other students on techniques. Not only does it transfer bad techniques on to the person they are advising but can be dangerous in a competition or should a street altercation occur.

Remember to always take your feedback with a grain of salt, absorb what is useful, and apply it to your life to grow your potential.

Chapter 16
Presence

IN THIS FINAL CHAPTER, I want to share with you a key component for driving excellence and success in individuals - the power of developing your presence. How you carry yourself through your non-verbal communication tells the world who you are as a person. Are you confident, happy, passionate, or are you low confident, sad, and lifeless?

Harvard professor Amy Cuddy in her famous TED talk spoke about the importance of our body language in how others perceive us. She found that people who exhibit power body language such as standing tall with their hands on the hips opening up their space will raise their testosterone levels thereby boosting their confidence. She added that when people exhibit this body language and pose, feel good hormones such as oxytocin are released into the blood stream giving you a sense of well-being.

In contrast, people who were in a slouched position, crossing their arms or sitting in a fetal position released cortisol, the stress hormone, thereby making them feel less confident.

In the animal kingdom, the alpha male shows dominance by taking up space. An alpha gorilla will stand tall making themselves appear larger. Other animals, when they feel threatened, will make themselves appear larger to ward off danger.

An interesting point Amy Cuddy also makes is how body language can also affect how we feel about ourselves. In other words, it can play a big part on changing our mind which is fascinating from a personal development standpoint.

According to studies, if we practice power posing for two minutes on a regular basis we can train our brain to make us feel more confident. Can our body language change our minds? The question now becomes will you feel fake or fraud? One of the things I struggled with as a child was wanting a sense of belonging. Being one of the few minorities in my neighborhood, I always felt like an outsider. I liked what Amy Cuddy suggested to combat this feeling of being a fraud while in the process of becoming what you want. She suggests using "fake it until you *become* it." I like this idea, that the road to excellence is a journey much like the road from white belt to black belt. One cannot just become a black belt no matter how much they feel like a black belt. However, one can begin the process by thinking like a black belt. Before Amy spoke about the value of power posing, I was unknowingly doing it at tournaments as I moved up in rank. Yes, it did make me feel good and confident about myself. Now thanks to her, there is scientific proof that power posing does help change our mindset.

I make great use of power posing before important events such as tournaments, interviews or speaking engagements.

Me and my opponent power posing before our match at the 2010 World Masters Nogi Brazilian Jiu-Jitsu Championships

If you want to champion your excellence, start holding your head up high like you belong. Make the practice of power posing a daily routine. Stand tall and be proud.

What Is Your Body Language Telling People?

"It's amazing what doors can open if you reach out to people with a smile, friendly attitude and a desire to make a positive impact."

– Richard Branson, Business magnate & philanthropist

When I was a teen I battled low self-confidence and body image issues. I was extremely self-conscious of myself. It wasn't until I started to take control of my life at the age of 26 that I noticed how important body language was in the way others perceive me, or how it dramatically changed my mindset for success. Although I had taken martial arts at a young age I didn't feel confident in my abilities as a fighter. I was extremely tentative and shy, fearing that failure would cause my father to lose respect for me. My reaction was to quit martial arts at age 16 to focus on track and field where my father wouldn't be able to have an influence.

Looking back at it now it was a mistake. My passion for the martial arts never waned. In fact, it grew during those years as I constantly read and thought about it every day. My problems did not go away, and for some reason bullies were able to spot me a mile away in a crowded room. Whether it was verbal or physical abuse, I did not have an option of defending myself. It was embarrassing to feel like the skinny guy in the classic Charles Atlas comic strip who gets sand kicked in his face by the bully. It is only when he builds some muscle that he was able to come back to teach the bully a lesson. Well I decided one day to complete that very comic strip in my life. Thank you to the Gracie family for Brazilian Jiu-Jitsu. It's been almost 13 years since I walked into the studio as a wide eyed white belt.

I never forgot the scared kid who buckled under pressure, who ran when things got tough, who walked with his head down, hiding in the corner of the classroom hoping to go unnoticed.

It's been refreshingly liberating to feel alive, free, confident, and to smile every day and to be able to take those painful childhood experiences and the struggles and help others right their own ship.

When I stand now before a class of 40 students, all looking at me with respect, it not only warms my heart to truly make a difference in their life, but I have to pinch myself every night before I go to sleep, telling myself there is so much more for me to achieve. Let's not stop there. Ask yourself what you can do better tomorrow to make your life one worth remembering.

WANT TO LEARN MORE ABOUT THE HUMAN EXCELLENCE PROJECT?

Raz Chan International offers a complete range of learning resources and coaching services to help you realize your greatest potential in career, health, and life.

"Inspire Yourself...Impact the World."

Visit **www.razchan.com**. to book your free 30 minute strategy session. Stay in touch with the latest blog articles on personal development, fitness, and wellness. You can also receive free weekly tips and have access to audio learning programs, books, and other resources.

▶ **Success coaching program designed for all those individuals who:**
- Feel stuck.
- Want to be successful.
- Want to be healthier.

▶ **The Black Belt Leader Executive Health Coaching consists of:**
- One-on-one personal service via online platforms.
- Offered once a week for the duration of the contract agreement.
- Based on the person's needs, desires and commitment to the program.

▶ **Corporate Workshops:**
- Improve employee performance, work satisfaction, health, and communication skills.
- Half day and full day sessions as well as Lunch and Learn formats to fit into the work day.

▶ **Speaking Engagements:**
- Motivate your employees and members at your next conference or event.
- Presentations are inspiring and relatable to the audience that can be applied to help them attain excellence.

For details and scheduling information visit www.razchan.com
or email raz@razchan.com

The Human Excellence Project

SUPPORT YOUTH AFTER SCHOOL PROGRAMS

Part proceeds from the sale of this book are donated to after school programs for underprivileged youth such as the Adopt-A-School, YMCA Strong Kids program, and The Boys and Girls club.

The funds help support youth sports, breakfast programs, and leadership programs. In buying this book, you are contributing in helping underserved youth succeed as adults.

ADOPT A SCHOOL

When kids come to school hungry, they can't concentrate on their lessons. Breakfast programs funded by your donations to Adopt a School help hundreds of children start the day with a nutritious meal.

Learn more about the Strong Kids program or contribute at www.vansunkidsfund.ca

THE YMCA STRONG KIDS PROGRAM

YMCA Strong Kids is an annual fundraising campaign focused on raising much needed resources to support proven YMCA programs that give kids the opportunities they need to reach their full potential: to live healthier, happier lives today, and grow into productive adults in the future.

Learn more about the Strong Kids program or contribute at www.ymcastrongkids.ca

BOYS AND GIRLS CLUB

The mission of all Boys and Girls Clubs in Canada is to provide a safe, supportive place where children and youth can experience new opportunities, overcome barriers, build positive relationships and develop confidence and skills for life.

Learn more about the Boys and Girls Club or contribute at www.bgccan.com

WE WANT TO HEAR FROM YOU

Now that you have finished reading The Human Excellence Project: Lessons Even Awesome Parents Never Teach, I want to hear from you. Share your thoughts and feedback about the book or a testimonial. You can connect with us through my website listed below.

Scan QR Code above or visit our website

www.razchan.com

P.S. Don't forget to request your FREE 30-minute one-on-one Success Life Coaching session. In addition, if you are a busy executive looking to lose weight or live a healthier lifestyle I also offer the Black Belt Leader Executive Health Coaching program.

The Human Excellence Project

ABOUT THE AUTHOR

"YOUR LEGACY WILL NEVER DIE"

–CARLOS GRACIE

RAZ CHAN IS A HUMAN EXCELLENCE coach, author, speaker, and Brazilian jiu-jitsu black belt. His expertise in the field of personal development, health and fitness has made him a highly sought after coach in helping individuals uncover their highest potential. He has co-authored a book with world renown personal development expert Brian Tracy.

As a child, his father lost his business to bankruptcy. The family spent many years struggling to make ends meet.

Unhealthy, and struggling with self-confidence as a youth, Raz discovered the power of self-development at the age of 26, transforming his daily destructive lifestyle to successful habits. In 2005, he left the corporate world to start his own fitness and personal development company.

Today, he spends the majority of his time coaching corporations, athletes, and entrepreneurs on maximizing their potential and health. Raz has been featured in major media outlets such as The New York Times, CTV, Vancouver Sun, Canada's Fashion Magazine, and Canada's Fight Network. He is also a 2x world masters silver medalist in Brazilian Jiu-jitsu.

In his spare time, he dedicates to helping feed kids from disadvantaged homes. In his opinion, no child should be held back from succeeding due to economic circumstances. His mission is to spread his message of incorporating 30 minutes per day working on personal excellence to the lives of every person in the world.

He is married, a proud papa to his Yorkie dog Max, and resides in Vancouver, Canada.

The Human Excellence Project